M000165914

THE QUR'ANIC WORLDVIEW:
A SPRINGBOARD FOR CULTURAL REFORM

THE QUR'ANIC WORLDVIEW:

A SPRINGBOARD FOR CULTURAL REFORM

ABDULHAMID A. ABUSULAYMAN

THE INTERNATIONAL INSTITUTE OF ISLAMIC THOUGHT
LONDON • WASHINGTON

© The International Institute of Islamic Thought, 1432AH/2011CE

The International Institute of Islamic Thought
P.O. BOX 669, HERNDON, VA 20172, USA
www.iiit.org

LONDON OFFICE
P.O. BOX 126, RICHMOND, SURREY TW9 2UD, UK
www.iiituk.com

*This book is in copyright. Subject to statutory exception
and to the provisions of relevant collective licensing agreements,
no reproduction of any part may take place without
the written permission of the publishers.*

ISBN 978-1-56564-365-9 PAPERBACK
ISBN 978-1-56564-366-6 HARDBACK

The views and opinions expressed in this book are those of the author and not necessarily those of the publisher. The publisher is not responsible for the accuracy of URLs for external or third-party internet websites referred to in this publication, and does not guarantee that any content on such websites is, or will remain, accurate or appropriate.

Typesetting and cover design by Sideek Ali
Printed in Malta by Gutenberg Press Ltd

To the sons of Islam, to the sons of man, a hope and a prayer that the Muslim community and humanity at large might recapture the primordial Islamic vision, the worldview that encompasses human accountability before the Divine both individually and collectively: a vision of 'power in the service of truth,' a vision of justice and charity, a vision of striving, creativity, and giving, a vision of knowledge and globalism, a vision of pride and dignity, a vision of brotherhood and solidarity, a vision of compassion, security, and peace...

A hope and prayer for coming generations that are diligent and capable, that lead the procession of pioneering leadership, that rescue the spirit of humanity, guiding it toward the horizons of brotherhood and justice, and bringing us soon to the shores of security and peace.

A hope and a prayer to the Most Compassionate, Who hears our pleas.

CONTENTS

The Qu'ran

Verily, this Qur'an shows the way to all that is most upright,...
(*sūrah al-Isrā'*, 17:9)

Say: "If all mankind and all invisible beings would come together with a view to producing the like of this Qur'an, they could not produce its like even though they were to exert all their strength in aiding one another!"
(*sūrah al-Isrā'*, 17:88)

...A divine writ [is this – a revelation] which We have bestowed upon thee from on high in order that thou might bring forth all mankind, by their Sustainer's leave, out of the depths of darkness into the light: onto the way that leads to the Almighty, the One to whom all praise is due.
(*sūrah Ibrāhīm*, 14:1)

For, indeed, We did convey unto them a divine writ which We clearly, and wisely, spelled out – a guidance and a grace unto people who will believe.
(*sūrah al-Aʿrāf*, 7:52)

The Hadith

ʿAlī ibn Abī Ṭālib (RAA)[1] related that the Messenger of God (ṢAAS)[2] had said, "There will be temptations." "What will be the way out of them, O Messenger of God?" ʿAlī asked. "The Book of God," he replied. "In it there are reports of events in the times that preceded you, as well as of events that will take place after you. It contains precepts on the basis of which to judge amongst yourselves, and which are to be taken with the utmost seriousness.... It is the rope of God that will not break, it is a tiding full of wisdom, it is the straight path. It is the source of guidance by virtue of which one's passions will not go astray and one's tongue will speak the truth without ambiguity. Scholars never get their fill of it, nor does it wear out from overuse. Its wonders never cease, and it contains the words which, when the jinn heard them they exclaimed, '...Verily, we have heard a wondrous discourse, guiding towards consciousness of what is right; and so We have come to believe in it...' (*Sūrah al-Jinn*, 72:1-2). Those who utter its words speak truth, those who act on it are rewarded, those who base their judgments on it carry out justice, and those who call others to it guide them to the straight path."[3]

1 RAA: *Raḍiyā Allāhu ʿanhu* (May God be pleased with him).
2 ṢAAS: *Ṣallā Allāhu ʿalayhi wa sallam* (May God's blessings and peace be upon him).
3 Narrated by al-Tirmidhī.

FOREWORD

THE International Institute of Islamic Thought (IIIT) has great pleasure in presenting Dr. AbdulHamid AbuSulayman's study, *The Qur'anic Worldview: A Springboard for Cultural Reform* which forms the English translation of the author's Arabic original, *al-Ru'yah al-Kawniyyah al-Ḥaḍāriyyah.*

This is a carefully reasoned, reflective work, the chief aim of which is to explore the reasons for the deteriorating state of the Muslim world and to address one of the central questions facing Muslims today – how to reverse the decline into which they have fallen and recover the brilliance of Islam's once great civilization. Looking back at the various stages of Islamic historical development, the author puts forward a solution that focuses on the recovery of what is termed, the Qur'anic worldview. It was the strict internalization of this perspective and close adherence to the principles of the Qur'an which, he contends, played a key factor in galvanizing the early fledgling Muslim community to achieve the successes that they once did, the profound impact of which is felt to this day. The rebirth of Islamic identity through this Qur'anic worldview, insists the author, is the key requirement of our times and a prerequisite for any future healthy and viable development of the Ummah.

Where dates are cited according to the Islamic calendar (hijrah) they are labelled AH. Otherwise they follow the Gregorian calendar and labelled CE where necessary. Arabic words are italicized except for those which have entered common usage. Diacritical marks have been added only to those Arabic names not considered modern.

The IIIT, established in 1981, has served as a major center to facilitate sincere and serious scholarly efforts based on Islamic vision, values and principles. Its programs of research, seminars and conferences during the last thirty years have resulted in the publication of more than four hundred titles in English and Arabic, many of which have been translated into several other languages.

We would like to express our thanks to Thomas Goldberg for the quality of his editorial work as well as the editorial and production team at the IIIT London Office and all those who were directly or indirectly involved in the completion of this work.

IIIT London Office
June 2011

PREFACE

THE question of what worldview one embraces is, whether consciously or unconsciously, a pivotal issue for every individual and every community, since it goes to the heart of who we are, the meaning and purpose of our existence, and what moves us to action in the world. The sounder and more positive one's worldview and the greater one's conscious awareness of it, the clearer will be one's sense of identity, and the more dynamism, positive energy, and creativity will be at one's disposal for the building of a healthy human civilization, in which life's true meaning and its sublime, God-given purpose are lived out.

Never in history has a nation lived creatively, purposefully, and constructively unless by virtue of the dynamism of its vision of itself and the world around it. Conversely, never in history has a nation grown backward and ossified, eventually disintegrating and falling into oblivion, but that it has done so as a result of the passivity and distorted nature of its worldview.

Through a penetrating, comprehensive review of the Muslim community's worldview and the stages through which it has passed over time, this book identifies one of the most fundamental reasons for the advancement of Muslim civilization in its early years. At the same time, it reveals important aspects of the distortion that has effected the Muslim community's perceptions and the resultant dangers it now faces. I set out to describe how this worldview can be recovered in such a way that the Muslim community and its individual members can recapture the positive dynamism of their past, thereby rescuing Muslim civilization and, along with it, human civilization in its entirety.

INTRODUCTION TO THE ARABIC EDITION

GIVEN all the works I have published to date, one might wonder what would have motivated me to write this extended reflection on the Islamic worldview at this particular point in time. In 1960, at which time I was doing my master's degree in political science at the University of Cairo, I wrote a book entitled *Naẓariyyat al-Islām al-Iqtiṣādiyyah: al-Falsafah wa al-Wasā'il al-Muᶜāṣirah* (The Islamic Theory of Economics: Philosophy and Contemporary Means). This was followed in 1987 by the publication of my *Towards an Islamic Theory of International Relations: New Directions for Methodology and Thought,*[1] in which I apply the same methodology that gave rise to my book, *Naẓariyyat al-Islām al-Iqtiṣādiyyah*. The theory expounded in this book led me to an understanding of texts and the Islamic heritage in a way that has yielded perspectives that could not have emerged through the methods applied in traditional Islamic studies. The method I have employed in my treatment of the theory of international relations – in the context of which I seek to adhere to an approach that is as objective, unbiased, inductive, and disciplined – is based on the texts and higher intents of the Islamic revelation, the wisdom embodied in the application of this revelation during the days of the Prophet Muhammad and the era of the rightly guided caliphs, as well as contemporary studies of human nature, both individual and collective, and the laws of the universe.

Even as a youth being schooled in the holy city of Makkah, the crisis resulting from the Muslim community's ongoing decadence and backwardness was a major concern for me. These phenomena were on the order of a riddle that captured my attention and fired my imagination. There being in a house as large and quiet as ours no enjoyment greater or diversion more inviting than that of reading. I would spend long hours in our vast library, which was well-stocked with books on

Islamic history and tradition as well as works by leading contemporary thinkers.

These experiences led me eventually to the study of political science. In 1986, I published *Azmat al-ʿAql al-Muslim* (Crisis in the Muslim Mind), which brought together the fruits of my thought and experience over the years. In this book, I reexamine many of the issues treated earlier in the book *Islāmiyyat al-Maʿrifah: Al-Khiṭṭah wa al-Injāzāt* (The Islamization of Knowledge: Plan and Achievements),[2] which sets forth the points of departure for the International Institute of Islamic Thought's (IIIT's) message and mission and the results of the Institute's international conference in Islamabad on the Islamization of knowledge, the Muslim mindset, and scientific research. Some of the issues I reexamine in *Crisis in the Muslim Mind* touch on the areas of childrearing and education, both of which were focuses of Dr. Faruqi's interest and concern.

During my years at King Saud University, the International Symposium, and the IIIT, I taught in the university, participated in Muslim youth activities, and explored issues relating to Islamic thought. I also spent ten years at the International Islamic University, Malaysia (IIUM), where I worked toward fulfilling IIIT's vision of reform in the realms of thought and emotion. I attempted to confront the crisis in Islamic thought through the unification of Islamic knowledge on the level of texts, vision, values, concepts, society, and day-to-day life. In so doing, I sought to help Muslims live in accordance with their God-given pristine human nature and the laws of the universe since, as I see it, only in this way will we be able to resolve the crisis in the Muslim will and heart, a crisis that begins in a child's emotional and spiritual upbringing, and which needs to be addressed through a focus on parental nurture and related programs and literature.

It was with such aims in mind that the IIUM adopted a double major track comprised of dual specializations in Islamic studies and social studies. It developed three new courses entitled, 'The Family and Parenting,' 'Creative Thinking and Problem-Solving,' and 'The Rise and Fall of Civilizations.' In addition, it developed two new diploma programs in the Education Department to prepare instructors who would be qualified to offer these courses in the Department of

Psychology, the Faculty of Islamic Revealed Knowledge and Human Sciences. These measures were taken with a view to making the aforementioned courses into requirements for all students regardless of their particular majors. In this way, students would be prepared to become model parents capable of raising a generation free of distorted educational, behavioral, intellectual, and doctrinal concepts and practices.

Another step taken by the IIUM was to establish a school that would encompass preschool-through-secondary education. This school that would offer instruction to both boys and girls, would operate under IIUM's supervision and management, and would serve, through the direction and content of its curriculum and activities, as a testing ground for IIUM's proposed educational philosophy.

In addition to the school's uniquely developed study materials and its Islamic-based architectural layout, which is designed to meet students' needs in the most ideal manner throughout the stages of their educational journeys – contact between the sexes is regulated in such a way as to achieve Islamic social, ethical, and educational aims. The school seeks to provide children with a balanced environment and sound social and psychological growth at the various stages of their development. From preschool through third grade, boys and girls study together, after which they are segregated in the classroom but continue to mix during free periods and in a variety of out-of-class activities. In this way, boys and girls experience a combination of segregation and integration. In cases in which the number of students is small, classes might continue to be mixed even past third grade; however, boys and girls are separated spatially in the classroom in order to prevent distraction, since it is at this stage of their development that children begin to become aware of the distinction between them and the opposite sex. Similarly, at this stage, children tend to gravitate toward members of their own gender in relating to the opposite sex.

During the middle school phase (seventh to ninth grades), girls and boys are segregated so as to avoid distraction in the classroom, and in order not to provide conditions that would be conducive to the occurrence of sexual contact. Such measures are deemed necessary in view of children's natural, but uninformed, curiosity and the likelihood of their making attempts to discover more about the other gender and satisfy sexual urges with one another before having arrived at a genuine awareness of the responsibilities attendant upon sexual relations and the dangers it can pose when engaged in irresponsibly. Such dangers have been observed particularly in liberal societies, especially at this stage of young people's development – which, if not understood correctly, can lead to highly undesirable consequences, including teen pregnancy and all this entails by way of negative effects on those involved.

The sexes continue to be separated throughout secondary school, which is the most critical phase of all, marked as it is by a kind of rashness and readiness to take risks resulting from teenagers' growing sense of autonomy and tendencies to rebel, not to mention the physiological changes they are experiencing and the sexual and psychological tensions these produce.

At the university level, classes become integrated once again, though male and female students are required to sit on separate sides of the lecture hall. Male and female students have the opportunity to meet during breaks and in eating areas. At the same time, there are girls-only halls reserved for female students, who wish to keep to themselves at any time. The IIUM encourages its male students to marry female classmates; in fact, it offers financial assistance to those who wish to do so, and it encourages students' parents to support their children in such situations. Consequently, there are growing numbers of marriages taking place between the IIUM's male and female students. This manner of arranging contact between the sexes, side by side with education and consciousness-raising through courses such as 'The Family and Parenting,' social and cultural activities that include both male and female students, as well as segregated activities such as sports, has led to a very low incidence of 'problems' in the sexual area, and those situations in which such mistakes have occurred have generally ended in marriage for the parties involved.

After completing my assigned task at the IIUM in 1999, I went back to full-time volunteer work, along with colleagues with whom I had founded the Muslim Students' Association and the IIIT. It was during this period that I devoted myself to the writing of *Azmat al-Irādah wa al-Wijdān al-Muslim* (Crisis in the Muslim Will and Emotions), whose central focus is the issue of emotional and spiritual education. My reflections and experiences over the years had led me to the conviction that knowledge of the right thing to do is no guarantee that we will do it – just as knowledge of what is wrong is no guarantee that we will avoid it unless the individual's emotional and spiritual orientation is according to reason and appropriate values in the direction of what reason affirms.

The Qur'anic account concerning the people of Israel provides support for this conviction. We find, for example, that God Almighty sent the Prophet Moses to deliver the people of Israel, who had been oppressed and enslaved by the pharaohs. In keeping with God's will to rescue them and bestow His blessings upon them, Moses led them out into Sinai, where God revealed on the tablets of the Sacred Law "...all manner of admonition..." (*sūrah al-Aʿrāf,* 7:145). However, their thinking became corrupted and distorted over time. Consequently, God destined them to wander in the wilderness of Sinai for forty years in order to correct their way of thinking, which had been warped through their years of slavery, and in order to raise up a generation of capable, free, strong men and women. It was only then that David could slay Goliath (*sūrah al-Baqarah,* 2:251), and that "...a small host [became able to] overcome a great host by God's leave!..." (*sūrah al-Baqarah,* 2:249).

During my own journey of the spirit and mind, I have found that whenever I am confronted with an issue or question that causes me confusion, anxiety, or uncertainty, the most helpful thing to do is to examine it carefully from an academic, sociological perspective. This involves dealing with the divinely revealed texts in a comprehensive manner, which includes a consideration of their overall context and message. In every case I encounter, I find that the application of these texts' higher intents, concepts, values, and principles in a concrete, realistic, scientific manner yields perspectives, insights, guidance, and wisdom that accord perfectly with human beings' current level of knowledge, as well as our era's particular possibilities, needs, and challenges.

The fruit of these systematic applications was the writing and publication of a number of academic works, including *al-ʿUnf wa Idārat al-Ṣirāᶜ al-Siyāsī fī al-Fikr al-Islāmī: Bayn al-Mabda' wa al-Khayār* (Violence and the Management of Political Conflict in Islamic Thought: Between Principle and Choice), *al-Insān bayna Sharīᶜatayn* (Man Between Two Laws); an Occasional Paper entitled, *Marital Discord: Recapturing Human Dignity Through the Higher Objectives of Islamic Law*; a lengthy article entitled, 'Legally Prescribed Punishments in Islam: Constants and Variables,' and another article entitled, 'Ishkāliyyat al-Istibtād wa al-Fasād fī al-Fikr wa al-Tārīkh al-Siyāsī al-Islāmī.' In the last-named work, in which I seek to present a new approach to political reform and Islamic governance, I attempt to explain why, if Islam is based on justice, we still encounter so much corruption and deviance in Arab-Muslim regimes and elsewhere in the life of Muslim societies.

My purpose in recounting the foregoing is to clarify the various dimensions of my personal experience and to convey the intensity with which I have grappled with these issues from the time I was young. Eventually, however, this experience crystallized in the form of my first book, *Naẓariyyat al-Islām al-Iqtiṣādiyyah,*[3] which was followed by a writing career that extended half a century.

And now, as my time on earth nears its end and my productive capacity wanes, I continue to face difficult questions and issues. However, I find that the 'crisis of thought and method' points toward an approach that will lead to sound thinking. Similarly, I find that the 'crisis in the Muslim will and emotions' may help us to identify the difficulties created by current educational approaches and practices in the Muslim community and its members' psychological and emotional makeup. At the same time, it points to the way we may be able to bring an end to misguided practices and approaches to human nurture and correct the manner in which we nurture young Muslims' minds and emotions.

However, merely grasping a sound way of thinking or method of childrearing or education will not suffice to overcome the backwardness to which the Muslim community has succumbed. Rather, we need to bring it out of the slough of marginalization and passivity into the realm of dynamism, movement, pioneering action, and initiative – thereby helping it realize the reform and progress which are its mission, and of which it is both capable and worthy. It is not enough for people to have a tool in their hand if they are unaware of the purpose for which they have it. For if the mere possession of the tool were sufficient to move Muslims to action, they would have acted by now – possessed as they are of abundant resources, and all the means necessary to enter the race, to exhibit their creative capacities, and to excel.

The Islamic world preceded many countries – including Japan, China, Russia, and others – in realizing the challenges posed by the progress of Europe at large, and how to address them. Nevertheless, many nations have managed not only to catch up with the West but even to surpass many Western countries in the realm of creativity, innovation, and material achievements. As for the Islamic peoples, one finds that despite all their breathless admiration for the West and conformity to the West in all aspects of life – be they civil or military, economic, or political – they have achieved nothing but a superficial simulation while, at the same time, falling ever more steadily into backwardness and neglect.

After centuries of failed attempts at imitation and simulation, it has become clear that no matter how available the means may be or how intense the suffering, nothing will change unless Muslims develop a worldview that can give them a genuine sense of the meaning and purpose of their existence and, in this way, serve as a motive force for positive, constructive action and reform. In other words, without a positive worldview, which provides a sense of purposefulness and motivation, the Muslim community will remain static. Machines and tools, threats and exhortations, no matter how abundant or well-stated, will be of no use to the community's well-being. One might liken the Muslim community to a machine that has been disassembled into its component parts. Even if every one of these parts happens to be of great value and in perfect condition, none of them will be able to perform its function or contribute to any sort of productivity as long as it is viewed in isolation from the entire entity of which it is a part.

In this connection, one notes the situation of the tens of thousands of Muslims who have earned higher degrees in academic research and various branches of education, but whose knowledge, tools, and technical skills have done nothing to move the Muslim community forward to more positive, constructive action. This is because movement and action are products of vision, purpose, and motivation. He who has no vision, purpose, or aim will never get anywhere no matter how abundant his store of information, tools, or mechanisms.

The question now is: have my discussions of the crises relating to Muslim educational methods and ways of thinking been a waste of time? Would it have been better had I begun with the study of the Qur'anic worldview and its various expressions rather than beginning, as I have, with issues of thought and method, will and emotions, and their manifestations? In answer to this question, I can only say that had I not already been steeped, albeit unconsciously and incompletely, in the Qur'anic worldview with all the benefits it has to offer us in our daily lives and in our pursuit of a wholesome civilization – it would not have been possible for me to address the issues of thought, method, will, and emotion to begin with. Nor would I have been able – without having first studied, analyzed, and traced the development of the issues of thought, method, and education – to perceive the hidden aspects of the Islamic worldview and observe the ways in which it has been distorted, nor to see how this distortion has influenced the course of Muslim thinking and feeling. Hence, what we have is a cycle of influences and counterinfluences, all of which need to be recognized in order for us to arrive at clarity, understanding, and sound applications.

Be that as it may, after having grappled with the issue of the Qur'anic worldview and its implications for human culture and civilization, I was gratified to discover that I could now offer convincing answers to a number of fundamental questions that had preoccupied and troubled me for so long. Such questions have to do with my understanding of myself, the meaning of my existence, my relationship with God, with others – and with the principles, concepts, and values that function as the tools and mechanisms by means of which the Islamic worldview can be translated into a concrete reality in our lives. Moreover, it is through the concretization of this worldview that we, as human beings, are able to achieve happiness, contentment, and peace of mind. As God Almighty says to those who have sought His favor, "O thou human being that hast attained to inner peace! Return thou unto thy Sustainer, well-pleased [and] pleasing [Him]: enter, then, together with My [other true] servants – yea, enter thou My paradise!" (*sūrah al-Fajr*, 89:27–30). This, undoubtedly, is the outcome that can be hoped for in both this world and the next by those who embrace and seek to live by the effective, rightly guided vision, which the Qur'an presents us.

Lastly, it is my hope that reform-minded thinkers and leaders will interact fruitfully with the subject of the Qur'anic worldview by studying it with the thoroughness it merits, and by instilling it – through childrearing, education, and professional training – in the hearts and minds of the Muslim community's sons and daughters. Only in this way, I believe, will we be able to produce both wholesome individuals and wholesome institutions through whose initiatives the Muslim community will rise and bear its message to the world – succeeding, prospering, and producing a civilization imbued with justice, brotherhood, solidarity, compassion, security, and peace. "...On that day will the believers [too, have cause to] rejoice in God's succour: [for] He gives succour to whomever He wills, since He alone is Almighty, a Dispenser of grace" (*sūrah al-Rūm*, 30:4–5).

Through God comes all true success. On Him do we rely,
and it is He who hears and answers our supplications.
Praise be to God, The Lord and
Cherisher of the worlds.

AbdulHamid AbuSulayman
Riyadh, 8/8/1429, 10/8/2008

CHAPTER I

THE QUR'ANIC WORLDVIEW AND HUMAN CULTURE

The Qur'anic Worldview as the Foundation for Reform

EVERY cultural system is associated with an underlying worldview which is translated into action by means of a particular way of thinking or mindset. Similarly, every way of thinking is associated with guiding principles that serve to define its outcomes. The clearer, the more positive, the more comprehensive, and the more flexible such a way of thinking is, and the more accurately it reflects the essence of its associated cultural system and worldview, the more effective and dynamic it will be. For this reason, increasing emphasis is being placed on the academic study of mindsets or ways of thinking – since, as I have noted, the fruits of a given cultural system, its effects, be they positive or negative, on the nations and peoples it governs, and its contributions to the progress (or regress) of humankind as a whole – are determined by this cultural system's underlying way of thinking.

One of the difficulties faced by those engaged in the study of cultural systems and their associated worldviews is that such systems and worldviews are sometimes marked by a degree of ambiguity and inconsistency. As a result, one may encounter contradictions between the theoretical premises on which such systems and worldviews are based, and the actual practices engaged in by the societies they have helped to form. It is essential that both a worldview and its associated way of thinking be positive, harmonious, and coherent. Consequently, those engaged in their study need to be aware of any and all imbalances or contradictions in a given worldview or its system of thought, since any flaw in either of them will diminish the effectiveness and vitality of the society or nation for which it serves as a guide, and will lead ultimately and inevitably to backwardness and cultural disintegration.

The principles, values, and concepts embodied in a given way of thinking both influence, and are influenced by, the worldview associated with this way of thinking. Such a way of thinking serves as the means by which a nation's worldview finds concrete expression in culture. Consequently, no way of thinking – including its component principles, values. and concepts – can be effective unless it is based on a soundly constructed, positive, coherent view of the world and culture whose foundations and aims are clearly defined and which has been instilled firmly in the minds and consciences of the society's members. This is the kind of worldview and way of thinking which can become a source of dynamism and well-being on both the individual and communal levels.

Throughout this work Islamic and Qur'anic worldview are used synonymously. The discussion of the Islamic worldview and its cultural implications must precede the discussion of the principles embodied in its associated way of thinking. Hence, I will begin by identifying the Islamic worldview as it pertains to culture, since it constitutes the roots out of which the Islamic way of thinking grows. It is the Islamic worldview, which determines and governs this way of thinking with its related principles, concepts, and values – as well as the goals and higher aims which they seek to fulfill. This worldview should be reflected in a cogent, coherent, scientific manner in the structure of an Islamic society's way of thinking, as well as in the ways in which this way of thinking is applied and the outcomes to which it leads.

Lack of awareness of the structure and content of the Islamic worldview – including the principles, values, and concepts which find concrete expression through its associated way of thinking – has caused this way of thinking to lose its vitality and resilience, robbing it of its centrality, relevance, and intellectual productivity. In other words, it has caused Islamic principles, concepts, and values to lose their influence over the way people think on the day-to-day level, and this despite the abundance of writings from the Islamic heritage at our disposal and the methodological tools we possess with which to understand this heritage.

The Muslims' way of thinking and their concepts and associated values have undoubtedly emerged from the Muslim community's Qur'anic worldview, since it is this view of the world which determines the way in which people – whether as individuals, nations, or a race – understand themselves, the meaning, purpose, and end of their existence, and their relationships to themselves, to others, to the world, and to the universe in all its dimensions. Hence, this worldview represents the motive force that defines the nature of the emotional and psychological energy that moves society and its individual members – determining their attitudes, their actions, and the trajectories of their lives, as well as the extent to which their lives contribute to cultural progress and its role in history.

Therefore, to the extent that this worldview is clear, consistent, positive, easy to understand, realistic, and down-to-earth, it will succeed in being a doctrinal force that forms people's psychological, spiritual, and intellectual lives in such a way that it moves them to positive, principled action both individually and communally. However, when such a worldview is vague, abstract, fanciful, and removed from reality, it reduces the nation's rich store of principles, concepts, and values to nothing but hollow words mouthed in assemblies and places of worship, or lengthy tomes held too sacred to be removed from the shelves where they sit gathering dust. As such, on the level of thought or social interaction, it will have little effect on individuals' lives or on the state of society.

There is, in the Muslim community, a lack of enlightened awareness and a lack of concern to make a thorough, studied examination of the Islamic worldview. This lack of awareness and concern are among the primary causes behind the perplexity, passivity, decline, disintegration, and backwardness which the Muslim community, both communally and individually, has suffered from increasingly over the last few centuries.

Muslim intellectuals' fascination with the competent, triumphant Western model because of its scientific and material achievements – together with the tendency among Western-educated Muslim thinkers to succumb to the spirit of receptivity and imitation rather than affirming confidence in their own heritage – has led Muslim intellectuals, whether consciously or unconsciously, to adopt a Western mentality along with its underlying worldview. Consequently, they have not been prone to make serious attempts at reforming Muslim thought patterns through the critical study and examination of their own tradition – and, most fundamentally, the Islamic worldview which has served in the past to renew the foundations of human civilization in ways that have made an indelible mark on human history. If they were, however, to undertake such a study, it would enable them to ascertain the reasons for the decline in adherence and application of the Islamic worldview and – with it, that of the decline of Islamic thought, social structure, and cultural standing.

Hence, unless Muslim intellectuals of all stripes and colors overcome their blind infatuation with Western ways, and unless Muslim educators and reformers undertake, seriously and with a spirit of objectivity and constructive criticism, to open the files of their own history and culture, they will never be able to effectively address the weakness, backwardness, and decline that have afflicted the Muslim community and marginalized its existence. It is important for such thinkers to realize that the first issue to which attention must be given is that of the primacy of the Islamic worldview and the failure to adhere to it, since herein lies the doctrinal foundation and the intellectual, psychological, and emotional impetus needed for the Muslim community to recover what it has lost.

The questions, then, which we need to address have to do, first, with the nature of the worldview appropriate for the Muslim community and its cultural system – and, second, with the reasons for this worldview's distortion and marginalization by Muslims, and the ways in which this distortion and marginalization have taken place.

How Did the Islamic Worldview Become Distorted?

To start with, we who are Muslims know about our glorious past, from the days of the Prophet to the early centuries of Islam with the Muslims' notable cultural achievements. Similarly, we are aware of the regrettable condition that prevailed during subsequent eras and which still prevails today. Consequently, the achievements witnessed during the days of the Prophet and the era of the rightly guided caliphs (Abū

Bakr the Righteous, and ʿUmar the Discerning) – the impeccable integrity and performance of their leaders, the unity and determination of their ranks, and the marvelous achievements by virtue of which new blood flowed through the arteries of human civilization – can only be explained with reference to the vital, effective view of the world and culture which such leaders possessed. This worldview imbued them with an enterprising spirit, dynamism, and an intellectual and emotional power that rendered them capable of accomplishments that dazzled their contemporaries. Moreover, the legacy of these people's historic feats lives on even now in the consciences and consciousness of the Muslim community. For the changes that were effected among the nations and peoples that came under Islamic rule did not stop at the levels of doctrine, culture, formalities, and attire; rather, they went beyond such things to encompass an unprecedented dimension – namely, that of language itself; for the tongues of these various peoples gave way to Qurayshite Arabic [the Quraysh were the ruling tribe of Makkah and the tribe to which the Prophet belonged], which became the language of the land wherever that uniquely influential generation set foot.

Hence, the question that we most need an answer to is: what are the features of the worldview that informed and guided that earlier generation, and how did this worldview come into existence? No less importantly, we need to know why and how, with the passing of the centuries, this worldview lost its influence, effectiveness, and dynamism to the point where the Muslim community of today has become weak, passive, and even persecuted.

However, before answering these questions and seeking to clarify the features of the Islamic, that is, the Qur'anic, worldview, it is important for us – given the radical changes reflected in our present situation – to distinguish the vision that guided the early generations of Muslims from the burdensome inheritance bequeathed to us by our latter-day ancestors. Judging from its visible effects, this modern-day worldview is for the most part a reactive theory, most of whose rhetoric consists of nothing but intimidation, reminiscence, allegations, dreams, and illusions that lay burdens on the Muslim's shoulders in an arbitrary, dictatorial fashion. Moreover, such a rhetoric of intimidation requires

Muslims to engage in a kind of 'self-negation' (as opposed to self-affirmation) in keeping with the dictates of this daunting, despotic, supremacist worldview.

A worldview and rhetoric of this nature tends to lead to a sense of oppression and defeat, passivity and marginalization, which leads in turn to a loss of drive and enthusiasm for the pursuit of knowledge and inspiration through the laws of the universe, for stewardship of the earth's resources, and for the improvement of human culture and civilization. Such a mentality can never yield anything but a passive, dependent, marginalized, oppressed, ineffective nation or community that lacks purpose, motivation, and passion. The members of such a community tend to be self-centered and to lack a spirit of solidarity, cooperation, and communalism. Hence, it comes as no surprise to find that the rhetoric of self-negation would be met with negative responses and with the tendency to resort to an unconscious defense of the self through a retreat into self-centeredness, hedonism, individualism, and passive introversion – a spiritual and psychological state reflected in the Qur'anic term *al-nafs al-ammārah bi al-sū'* (the self that "...incites [him] to evil..." *sūrah Yūsuf*, 12:53). In such a situation, the occasional flashes of desire to do good for others and excel in one's performance become nothing more than a token expression of the latent, God-given spiritual urges of the human conscience, or what the Qur'an refers to as *al-nafs al-lawwāmah* ("...the accusing voice of man's own conscience!" *sūrah al-Qiyāmah*, 75:2).

The Qur'anic worldview could only have achieved what it did in ages past because it was a positive, dynamic perspective that fostered the realization and affirmation of the self in its various individual and communal aspects. The motivation generated by love, positive desire, and conviction ("...those who have attained to faith love God more than all else...." *sūrah al-Baqarah*, 2:165) outweighs the effects of fear, intimidation, and passivity. In this way, human beings are able to achieve self-realization and come to understand the meaning of their lives through constructive action in the context of the human culture to which they belong. In so doing, they experience enthusiasm for their performance in life, both individually and communally, and on both the material and spiritual levels. When people live under the influence of the constructive Qur'anic worldview that prevailed in the early days of Islam, they begin to respond to their God-given spiritual longings just as they do to their physical urges and needs. In meeting their physical needs and urges, moreover, they do so not in response to temporal, selfish, aggressive, animal instincts (the self that "incites to evil") based on the desire to vanquish or to survive at others' expense – in which case 'might makes right,' and life is a matter of the survival of the fittest. Rather, they do so in ways that are consistent with their God-given spiritual nature based on the values of justice, charity, brotherhood, and peace in the broadest sense – in which case 'might serves right' in keeping with the inclinations of a God-inspired conscience.

God Almighty declares:

> And so, set thy face steadfastly towards the [one ever-true] faith, turning away from all that is false, in accordance with the natural disposition which God has instilled into man: [for,] not to allow any change to corrupt what God has thus created – this is the [purpose of the one] ever-true faith; but most people know it not. (*sūrah al-Rūm*, 30:30)

> This [message] is no less than a reminder to all mankind – to every one of who wills to walk a straight way. (*sūrah al-Takwīr*, 81:27–28)

> God does not burden any human being with more than he is well able to bear: in his favour shall be whatever good he does, and against him whatever evil he does. O our Sustainer! Take us not to task if we forget or unwittingly do wrong! O our Sustainer! Lay not upon us a burden such as Thou didst lay upon those who lived before us! O our Sustainer! Make us not bear burdens which we have no strength to bear!... (*sūrah al-Baqarah*, 2:286)

> Nay! I call to witness the Day of Resurrection! But nay! I call to witness the accusing voice of man's own conscience! (*sūrah al-Qiyāmah*, 75:1–2)

> But unto him who shall have stood in fear of his Sustainer's Presence, and held back his inner self from base desires, paradise will truly be the goal! (*sūrah al-Nāziʿāt*, 79:40–41)

> ...Verily, God does not change men's condition unless they change their inner selves;... (*sūrah al-Raʿd*, 13:11)

Ḥājib ibn al-Walīd related, on the authority of Muḥammad ibn Ḥarb, on the authority of al-Zubaydī, on the authority of al-Zuhrī, on the authority of Saʿīd ibn al-Musayyab, on the authority of Abū Hurayrah, who used to say, "The Messenger of God said, 'Everyone who comes into this world is born with his or her God-given nature. Then his or her parents make him or her into a Jew, a Christian or a Magian....'"[1]

In a hadith related by Wābiṣah ibn Maʿbad, we are told that he came to the Messenger of God, who said to him, "Wābiṣah, shall I tell you what you have come to ask me about?" "O Messenger of God," he replied, "Tell me!" And he said, "You have come to ask me about righteousness and unrighteousness." "That is correct," Wābiṣah replied. The Messenger of God then held his three fingers side by side and began scratching Wābiṣah's chest, saying, "Wābiṣah, ask yourself what righteousness and unrighteousness are. Righteousness is whatever sets your heart and soul at rest, while unrighteousness is whatever causes unrest in your heart and soul, even if others should tell you it is right."[2]

Clouds of ambiguity came gradually to settle over the Islamic worldview after the end of the Prophetic era and the days of the rightly guided caliphates. This process took place due to the gradual disappearance of the community of the Prophet's companions, who had been nurtured on the words of the Holy Qur'an under the tutelage of the original bearer of the Islamic message and its ideal proponent. It was these men who had witnessed and internalized the Prophet's example and the wisdom with which he had applied the Qur'anic vision, principles, and values to the concrete situations they faced in their own day. With the passage of time, the Companions' numbers began to dwindle through death. Some of them died natural deaths, while a good number of them met their ends on the battlefield due to the necessity of confronting the desert Arabs' uprising against Islamic rule following the Prophet's death. This was followed by the confrontation with the corrupt aggressor empires of the age – namely, the Persian Empire to the north and east and the Byzantine Empire to the north and west. It was this latter confrontation which made it necessary to draft the Arab tribes into the Muslim army of conquest at a time when they had yet to be fully educated in the Islamic message and mentality. As a result, the rebelling desert Arab tribes defeated the Muslim state's military force and undermined its political life. Given the fact that the desert Arabs were new to Islam, they were still under the influence of primitive racist tribal values and social traditions of the sort that exclude the Other. It would not have been possible entirely to erase the effects of such tribal mentalities – especially given the enormity of the conflicts imposed by the Byzantine and Persian Empires on the fledgling Islamic state, not to mention the harshness of desert life and long-standing tribal conflicts over scarce natural resources. All such factors served to hinder the absorption of the values of solidarity and metatribal thinking that underlie Islamic social institutions such as the family, brotherhood through nursing from the same woman, treaties of protection and safe-conduct, citizenship (the principles of which are set forth in the Charter of Madinah), and the concepts of state and nation. It is important for us to realize the significance of the fact that the desert Arabs were able to undermine the fledging Muslim nation's political life, as well as the fact that the political realm gained control over the religious, putting it to use for its own ends, an eventuality that led inevitably to tyranny and corruption. Many of the Prophet Muhammad's predictions concerning the future had to do with distortions and uprisings that were to take place and the perilous effect they would have on the course of the Muslim nation's economic, social, and political life. Even more importantly, such events would have a critical impact on the nation's intellectual life and on the Islamic worldview.

The desert Arab tribes inhabited an arid, barren environment, and lived an isolated existence in the Arabian peninsula's vast, mountainous deserts. Hence, prior to the coming of Islam, these tribes exhibited a kind of cultural incompetence or immaturity. Given this situation, the Islamic community and state had a duty to work for these tribes' human welfare by all available and appropriate means, and to integrate them into a civilized, cohesive, humane system free of racial prejudice. As the first phase in a process of cultural and social education, the fledging Muslim state sought to do just this by bringing the Bedouin into the newly developing Islamic society. Hence, although the

Messenger of God and Abū Bakr after him adhered to a policy of 'either Islam, or war,' the Arab desert tribes were not in actuality being coerced into embracing Islamic doctrine. Rather, this policy might better be likened to the approach required for wild horses that need to be bridled in order to be tamed and domesticated, or the firm approach needed for an unruly child: "The Bedouin say, 'We have attained to faith.' Say [unto them, O Muḥammad]: 'You have not [yet] attained to faith; you should [rather] say, "we have [outwardly] surrendered" – for [true] faith has not yet entered your hearts...."' (*sūrah al-Ḥujurāt*, 49:14).

It was not without reason that when the Bedouin tribes showed signs of retreating from the Islamic community of brotherhood, cooperation, and solidarity and returning instead to a life of desert wolves whose existence revolves around narrow tribal allegiances, conflict, aggression, highway robbery, plundering, and looting, and the principled Caliph Abū Bakr declared, "I swear by God, I will fight whoever distinguishes between prayer and zakah!" Hence, emphasis was not placed on doctrine and faith, but rather on ritual prayer and the payment of zakah, which served to form the spiritual and material building blocks by means of which the community could attain greater maturity, competence, social solidarity, and a sense of their responsibility as God's stewards on earth. Prayer, for example, helps to form a spiritual, doctrinal, emotional, and intellectual community that lends its members a sense of belonging. The organization and structure of such a community are characterized by coordinated, harmonious communal action and ritual which foster a spirit of brotherhood and equality without distinction based on one's tribal affiliation, race, color, language, or social standing. Similarly, zakah is an expression of the spirit of brotherhood and solidarity, which is necessary for the establishment of a truly human cultural community.

As for faith in the one God and in the message of peace, justice, compassion, human brotherhood, and purposeful, ethical stewardship, which was brought by the Prophet Muhammad from God Almighty – a message accompanied by various forms of worship of the just and merciful God, and which in turn involves willing self-surrender based on inward conviction to the disciplines of fasting, pilgrimage, and the pursuit of goodness, justice, excellence, and sincerity in all one's actions – knowledge, reasoned persuasion, and time will suffice to instill them consciously in people's hearts and minds.

The following verses from the Holy Qur'an illustrate the features of the Bedouin tribes' barbarism and primitive way of thinking. Through these words we get a sense of their immaturity and their need for social, cultural, and ethical instruction. Concerning these tribes, God Almighty states:

> How [else could it be]? – since, if they [who are hostile to you] were to overcome you, they would not respect any tie [with you,] nor any obligation to protect [you]. They seek to please you with their mouths, the while their hearts remain averse [to you]; and most of them are iniquitous. God's messages have they bartered away for a trifling gain, and have thus turned away from His path: evil, behold, is all that they are wont to do, respecting no tie and no protective obligation with regard to a believer; and it is they, they who transgress the bounds of what is right! Yet if they repent, and take to prayer, and render the purifying dues, they become your brethren in faith: and clearly do We spell out these messages unto people of [innate] knowledge! But if they break their solemn pledges after having concluded a covenant, and revile your religion, then fight against these archetypes of faithlessness who, behold, have no [regard for their own] pledges, so that they might desist [from aggression]. (*sūrah al-Tawbah*, 9:8–12)

> [The hypocrites among] the Bedouin are more tenacious in [their] refusal to acknowledge the truth and in [their] hypocrisy [than are settled people], and more liable to ignore the ordinances which God has bestowed from on high upon His Apostle – but God is All-Knowing, Wise. And among the bedouin are such as regard all that they might spend [in God's cause] as a loss, and wait for misfortune to encompass you, [O believers: but] it is they whom evil fortune shall encompass – for God is All-Hearing, All-Knowing. (*sūrah al-Tawbah*, 9:97–98)

> He it is who has sent unto the unlettered people an apostle from among themselves, to convey unto them His messages, and to cause them to grow in purity, and to impart unto them the divine writ as well as wisdom – whereas before that they were indeed, most obviously, lost in error; (*sūrah al-Jumʿah*, 62:2)

The Bedouin tribes' negative influence on Islamic political life began with the collapse of the rightly guided caliphate and the establishment of the ruthless Umayyad dynasty. The lingering effects of their primitive ways of thinking and racist approach to human relationships further obscured the Qur'anic worldview – which had been so splendidly incarnated in the lives of the Prophet and the Prophet's Companions, including both the Emigrants and the Supporters* – gradually supplanting it with a desert Arab worldview. This perspective was derived primarily from what one might term the 'mixed discourse' that had been addressed to them by the Messenger of God, who tempered the divine message to them in ways that took account of their particular circumstances, spiritual condition, and level of understanding. These extenuating factors can be discerned through what remained of their pre-Islamic traditions and narrow tribal allegiances, the descriptions of them in the Holy Qur'an and sayings of the Prophet predicting times of future unrest – as well as in the Prophet's warnings concerning the state in which the Muslim community would find itself after his departure due to the influence of the desert Arabs and other peoples who were to come under Islamic rule in the wake of the tremendous conflicts that would break out between the Islamic state and the hostile, corrupt empires surrounding the Arabian peninsula.

During the latter part of the era for which the Prophet left us an overall, predictive description, the desert Arab tribes and the Umayyad leadership did away with the rightly guided caliphate. During this period of time, the Qur'anic spirit was notably muted, while the prudent consultative approach of the first four caliphs was transmuted into a wicked, tyrannical regime in which power was passed on based on heredity alone. The city of Madinah was occupied; the Kaᶜbah was razed; and al-Ḥusayn ibn ᶜAlī and ᶜAbd Allāh ibn al-Zubayr were killed. Meanwhile, the Companions' successors and the school of thought that had served as the basis for the rightly guided caliphate were essentially eliminated, and the life of the mosque was isolated

---

*Supporters (Arabic: *Anṣār*) denotes the Madinan citizens that helped Prophet Muhammad and the *Muhājirūn* (Emigrants) on their arrival to the city after the migration to Madinah.

from the affairs of political life. The Companions' successors became little more than theorists whose role was restricted for the most part to the realm of worship in the narrow sense, affairs relating to the individual and the family, and legal rulings pertaining to contracts of sale and individual transactions. This development caused an attitude of dependency to make its way into the public and political spheres, while blurring and distorting many aspects of the Islamic worldview. As a consequence, religion came gradually to be employed in the service of political rulers and their devotees; public institutions suffered decline; tyranny was established as the rule of the day; and corruption and its attendant injustices reached alarming proportions in the political, the economic, and the social spheres alike.

By virtue of this noxious, pagan tribal legacy and the entry of new peoples into Islamic society, including what these peoples' cultures, worldviews, and heritages brought with them by way of traditions and ways of thought inherited from bygone civilizations that had gone bankrupt or died, having served their purpose in the history of human civilization – particularly the Greek civilization with its formal logic and mythically oriented doctrines – the intellectual and doctrinal confusion only grew worse. This, not surprisingly, produced even greater distortion in the Islamic worldview, which led in turn to further spiritual weakening in the Muslim community. The aforementioned developments were clearly observable by the end of the Umayyad era through the disintegration of the Islamic state's political system and a retreat from the fundamentals that had been revealed in the Holy Qur'an for the renewal of human civilization. Such fundamentals included the vision of a divinely granted stewardship, the purposefulness of creation, the rule-governed quality of human nature, the ethical foundations of human conduct, and the commitment to the principles of justice, brotherhood, the oneness of God, consultation, freedom, responsibility, and constructive action.

It is important for us to realize also that the aforementioned retreat from a properly Islamic vision of human beings' God-given purpose on earth could not have been corrected by the material prosperity that had been achieved over time, in large part due to the influx of skilled artisans and other professionals that had accompanied the Islamic conquests and territorial expansion. Nor could the facade of material success conceal the spiritual malaise that had overtaken Islamic culture and society in the form of corruption, institutional rigidity, and breakdown. The process of cultural, intellectual, and doctrinal distortion eventually reached crisis proportions: things had now reached the point where – given the ubiquity of fatalism, superstition, charlatanry, attempts to lend legitimacy to the status quo through distorted, truncated, and forged texts, and the growing influence of Jewish folklore and Gnostic or mystical beliefs – the Islamic worldview had all but been lost. Gone was the sense of purposefulness and motivation that had once driven the nation, and with it, progress, creativity, and constructive action. The resulting vacuum was filled by the rhetoric of subjugation and intimidation, which further reinforced people's sense of indifference and impotence. Conflict, fragmentation, backwardness, and institutional dysfunction were now so much the order of the day that the worn-out, ossified, corrupt, tyrannical regimes, which ruled throughout the Islamic empire, were – albeit with a few rare exceptions – no longer capable of protecting their subjects from exploitation, subjugation, and crushing defeat.

If we give careful thought to the course taken historically by Islamic thought, we will find that all the aforementioned factors – in particular the formalism of Greek thought and logic and the mythical bent of its doctrine and philosophy (features which ought to have been taken note of in order not only to benefit from their positive aspects, but in order to avoid their pitfalls as well) – had a notably deleterious effect on the course of Islamic thought in its doctrinal, intellectual, and cultural dimensions alike. Preoccupation with doctrinal, metaphysical, and theological sophistries exhausted the energies of Muslim scholars and philosophers – be they Muᶜtazilites, Asharites, Shiites, Sunnites, Sufis, or otherwise – while distracting the Muslim community from its true mission, namely, that of developing human civilization through creativity and the wise use of the human mind and material resources. Examples of such sophistic digressions include the controversy over the creation of the Qur'an, predestination vs. free will, and other issues emphasized by Scholastic philosophy, none of which was of any relevance to the way in which to administer human affairs.

The Conflict Between Revelation and Reason: Reality or Illusion?

The question of whether there is a conflict between revelation and reason is based on an illusion that has embroiled the Muslim community in a sophistic philosophical battle, which has no foundation either in human nature or objective reality. In fact, any inconsistency or conflict between revelation and human reason is an illusion, since the function of reason in this realm is, in essence, like that of a scale that undertakes the task of comparing and contrasting two sets of givens in order to determine the degree to which one balances the other out.

The two scales of the balance here are not reason and revelation themselves, but rather the written texts of the revelation (in Arabic, *al-naql*, literally, 'that which has been conveyed') on one hand, and the reality of human nature and the laws of the universe (*al-fiṭrah wa al-sunan*) on the other. The task of reason is to determine the extent to which there is agreement and harmony between revelation as that which has been conveyed to human beings (*al-naql*) and the God-given nature of things, both humanly and non-humanly speaking. In other words, reason's job is to verify that the revelation (that which is written, *al-masṭūr*) describes the reality of nature, both human nature and the wider universe (that which is observed, *al-manẓūr*).

From the foregoing it will be clear that the conflict, if such exists, cannot be between revelation and human reason, which is on the order of a scale for weighing things. However, one might envision the existence of such a conflict – on the theoretical level, at least, between revelation and nature – in which case, the function of reason is to investigate the relationship between the two of them and to ascertain whether it is a relationship of balance and mutual support, or one of discord and disagreement.

In the case of discord and disagreement, we are called upon to engage in scientific investigation, study, and examination so as to discover why the scale is giving the reading it is. In this way, one hopes to determine the reasons for the imbalance, where the truth lies, and what will serve everyone's best interest. Is there an inadequate understanding of the meaning of the revelation sent down by the Creator?

Or has there been a misunderstanding of human nature and the laws of the universe?[3]

Because both revelation and the laws of the universe come from the same source, there is no way that there could be any genuine inconsistency or discord between the actual meaning and guidance conveyed by divine revelation, and the true character of human nature, the laws of the universe, and their purposes. When examined in a scientific manner, revelation is seen to be entirely just and fair – being a reflection of true human nature and the laws of the universe, and a source of guidance for the purpose of human fulfillment and self-realization in the soundest, truest sense of these words. It is for this reason that God Almighty commands us, saying:

> And so, set thy face steadfastly towards the [one ever-true] faith, turning away from all that is false, in accordance with the natural disposition which God has instilled into man: [for,] not to allow any change to corrupt what God has thus created – this is the [purpose of the one] ever-true faith; but most people know it not. (*sūrah al-Rūm*, 30:30)

When viewed from this perspective, it can be seen that the pleasure experienced in marital union, striving for an honest living, the pursuit of beneficial knowledge, and martyrdom in defense of people's lives, wealth, and honor against those who would commit aggression against them, are all equally affirmations of God's love and ways of seeking His blessing and approval.

Under the influence of Greek formal logic, Muslims unwittingly fell prey to the fallacious notion that there is a conflict between reason and revelation. This development constituted a dangerous turning point in the course of Islamic thought and civilization. Moreover, until we realize the destructive impact this fallacy has had on Islamic thought and civilization, the Muslim community will never be able to regain its unity, its vision, its motivation, its pioneering spirit, or its scientific and cultural edge. And until it is able to recover these blessings, it will find no way to set human civilization anew on the path of justice, brotherhood, cooperation, progress, and peace.

The approach based on the Greeks' sophistic, mythical philosophy, and formal logic was, in essence, an academic luxury enjoyed by the 'free men' in power. As such, it had nothing to do with an understanding of reality, human nature, and the laws of the universe; nor did it bear any connection to research, reflection, and objective, scientific investigation of the realities of the cosmos for the purpose of populating and developing the earth and making good use of its resources. Rather, it was a self-absorbed system of thought steeped in myth and abstract reasoning, which did nothing but exhaust people's mental energy on useless concerns that had no basis in reality. Such a system of thought, which grew out of the subjective reflections, excesses, and delusions of the ruling class allowed numerous disparate visions and perspectives to arise, not because this was what the facts dictated, but rather due to the diversity of the whims and illusions of the society's leading thinkers. It was this that opened the door wide to a plethora of whimsical inclinations and designs, subjective perspectives and visions, all of which led in turn to needless, baseless discord and division. If only those embroiled in such disputes and divisions had appealed for solutions to the authentic, integral texts of the revelation, the facts of human nature and the laws of the universe, most of their disagreements would have faded away into nothing, and they would have come together as brethren in the unity of truth.

As such, reason is not a type of subject matter, but rather an instrument or tool without which it would not be possible for human beings to perceive, judge, or compare. After all, whenever a conflict of any sort arises, it is resolved through the use of reason, by means of which we assess the claim being made by examining it in relation to the facts at hand. Only in this way are we able to determine whether the claim being made is consistent with the objective facts. If, for some reason, we are unable to reach a conclusion, it indicates that the issue of concern calls for further examination and that more facts need to be gathered.

Something we should not lose sight of in this connection is that nowhere in the Qur'an do we find any mention of 'reason' or 'the mind' in and of itself. Indeed, the Arabic word which is rendered *reason* or *mind* (*al-ᶜaql*), is nowhere to be found in the Qur'an (The word *aql* appears in the Qur'an in its verb form *yaᶜqilūn* meaning "to apply reason" and not in its noun form meaning "discernment"). The reason for this is that rather than being a discrete entity, *al-ᶜaql* is, an instrument or tool by means of which human beings understand, compare, and draw connections between facts, patterns, and laws of the cosmos. Consequently, the issue of concern to human beings in relation to the mind, or reason, has to do not with reason itself or its axioms – since these are an unchanging aspect of human nature – but rather with the way in which reason and its capacities are put to use. When we reason, we are able to perceive reality and arrive at judgments concerning claims and assumptions in relation to facts and objective scientific laws. If the claims or assumptions under discussion are found to agree with the facts before us, they may be said to 'be correct.' Otherwise, we know there to be some flaw in our understanding that needs to be addressed through further research, thought, and investigation. This is why the Qur'an speaks so frequently of the processes of trying to understand (*al-tadabbur*) – using one's reason (*al-ᶜaql/al-taᶜaqqul*), reflection (*al-tafakkur*), and seeing (*al-ibṣār*).

Early Muslim scholars sometimes encountered situations in which their logical, linguistic understanding of Qur'anic texts conflicted with what was required in order to serve people's best interests. This happened most frequently in connection with newly arising circumstances, which were compared by way of analogy to texts dealing with similar situations that had arisen at an earlier time. Realizing that they did not possess sufficient knowledge or information to identify the errors in the analogies they had drawn, scholars would simply adopt an interpretation that was in keeping with the overall spirit of the Islamic law and which they saw as meeting the requirements of human welfare; in other words, they adhered to the practice of juristic preference (*istiḥsān*).

This approach developed into what came to be known as the discipline of *maqāṣid al-sharīᶜah* (the higher intents of Islamic law), which involves examining particulars in light of universals as a way of fulfilling the spirit of the Islamic law in concrete human situations. In this way, scholars were able to protect and uphold people's spiritual and material interests, which embodies the ultimate aim of the Islamic message: "O you who have attained to faith! Respond to the call of God and the Apostle whenever he calls you unto that which will give you life;..." (*sūrah al-Anfāl*, 8:24).

One of the primary reasons for the difficulty involved in drawing a valid analogy between a new situation and a text that applied originally to an earlier situation is that the element of place and time is not fully understood or taken into account, which causes the analogy drawn to be partial. Consequently, societal conditions are in a state of such constant flux that partial analogies are of no real benefit.

Be that as it may, it is impossible that there should be a genuine conflict between revelation in the sense of that which is written (*al-masṭūr*) and the realities of existence, or that which is observed (*al-manẓūr*). Nevertheless, apparent conflicts may arise when there is an inadequate understanding of either the revelation or the realities of existence. Hence, lest harm be done to people and their interests through a deviation from what is most just and beneficial, priority must be given to universals and higher intents until the source of the misunderstanding has been identified.

Human reason operates in much the same way as a computer in that its output is dependent on its input. If the input it receives is valid, its output will likewise be valid. Similarly, if one has the proper conceptualization or understanding of things and if the claims one makes are consistent with this conceptualization, one's actions will be an expression of reality and truth. If, on the other hand, the input one receives consists of sophistries, humbug, and caprice, the output likewise will be more sophistries, humbug, and caprice – and the human cultural enterprise will go the way of the wind. When this happens, the mind of the Muslim becomes preoccupied with useless superstition, trivial thought revolving around the minutiae of life and pointless philosophical wrangling like whether man is determined or free, or whether the Qur'an is created or not.

As revelation (*al-masṭūr*), the Qur'an is an expression of that God-given, integral human nature which is purposeful, constructive, and ethical, and of the laws and patterns revealed in the cosmos in which we live (*al-manẓūr*). Hence, the proper understanding of revelation cannot possibly require coercion, compulsion, or a negation of nature, be it human nature or the laws of the cosmos. Nor does it entail the imposition of burdens and obligations that are extraneous to the meaning of human existence. On the contrary, divine revelation came in order to lead us to an understanding of our own true nature and the nature of the creation as a whole. In this way, the Qur'an serves to guide our course in such a way that we achieve genuine self-realization – living in harmony with our God-given human nature and responding fully and rightly to our need to be responsible, productive stewards of what God has given us. For only in this way will we be able to build a just, healthy, creative society.

Hence, for example, when the Qur'an informs us that man was created as a vicegerent (that is, divinely commissioned steward) on earth, one who would inherit it (*sūrah al-Baqarah*, 2:30), it is not imposing this function on human beings as an additional burden that is not integral to who they are. Rather, it is simply calling our attention to this inborn aspect of our nature. For we are, in fact, qualified by virtue of our inborn capacities to undertake this function, and the revelation serves to guide us in its fulfillment by giving us the proper awareness of it. In this way, it enables us to achieve self-realization and to achieve genuine felicity in both this world and the next.

Similarly, the Qur'an affirms that human beings have been given a divine trust to bear (*sūrah al-Aḥzāb*, 33:72). In so doing, it is not assigning people a task that does not belong to the essence of what they were created to be. After all, the individual is aware within himself of both positive and negative spiritual propensities – some that impel him to seek reform and edification, others that lure him toward corruption and attachment to the merely physical or material; some inspire him to seek justice, while others tempt him to injustice; some summon him to the highest good, while others threaten to drag him into the abyss of evil. Moreover, everyone has the intuitive sense of possessing, albeit in limited measure, the ability to choose freely which of two alternative paths they will tread. Divine revelation urges human beings to activate and obey their will to do good and provides guidance to this end. Moreover, those who read the divine revelation know within themselves that what the revelation is urging them to do is right. At the same time, the revelation reassures us of the justice of God, who only requires of us what we are capable of and no more, since our responsibility is commensurate with our abilities, potential, and the knowledge and understanding at our disposal: "God does not burden any human being with more than he is well able to bear: in his favour shall be whatever good he does, and against him whatever evil he does..." (*sūrah al-Baqarah*, 2:286), and, "...We would never chastise [any community for the wrong they may do] ere We have sent an apostle [to them]" (*sūrah al-Isrā'*, 17:15).

When, for example, the Qur'an calls upon human beings to read (*sūrah al-ʿAlaq*, 96:1), it is not assigning us a task that is alien to our nature. After all, people had been reading prior to the time when the Qur'an was revealed, and they will go on reading as long as humanity exists for the simple reason that it is in their nature to do so. Without reading and writing in their various forms, human beings would not be equipped for the task of vicegerency and stewardship, nor would they be capable of developing advanced civilizations. Reading, which is necessarily accompanied by recording and writing, is a fundamental, instinctive means of establishing, nurturing, and preserving human culture from one generation to the next. The Qur'an affirms human beings as 'reading' creatures by commanding them to, 'Read!' In so doing, it calls this essential aspect of our nature to our attention and brings it to the center of our awareness. At the same time, this affirmation in the form of a command is meant to guide this human capacity of ours in such a way that we will use it for the good, and that its use will be motivated by faith, wisdom, and a sense of ethical purposefulness:

> ...Our Sustainer is He who gives unto every thing [that exists] its true nature and form, and thereupon guides it [towards its fulfillment]. (*sūrah Ṭā Hā*, 20:50)

> Read in the name of thy Sustainer, who has created – created man out of a germ-cell! Read – for thy Sustainer is the Most Bountiful One who has taught [man] the use of the pen – taught man what he did not know! Nay, verily, man becomes grossly overweening whenever he believes himself to be self-sufficient: for, behold, unto thy Sustainer all must return. (*sūrah al-ʿAlaq*, 96:1–8)

> And lo! Thy Sustainer said unto the angels: "Behold, I am about to establish upon earth one who shall inherit it." They said: "Wilt Thou place on it such as will spread corruption thereon and shed blood – whereas it is we who extol Thy limitless glory, and praise Thee, and hallow Thy

name? " [God] answered: "Verily, I know that which you do not know." And He imparted unto Adam the names of all things; then He brought them within the ken of the angels and said, "Declare unto Me the names of these [things], if what you say is true." They replied: "Limitless art Thou in Thy glory! No knowledge have we save that which Thou hast imparted unto us. Verily, Thou alone art All-Knowing, Truly Wise." Said He: "O Adam, convey unto them the names of these [things]." And as soon as [Adam] had conveyed unto them their names, [God] said, "Did I not say unto you, 'Verily, I alone know the hidden reality of the heavens and the earth, and know all that you bring into the open and all that you would conceal'?" (*sūrah al-Baqarah*, 2:30–33)

It will be clear from the foregoing that in the Qur'anic worldview, there is no possibility of genuine conflict between revelation on one hand, and the facts of nature, both human and cosmic, on the other. Hence, all that is required of the searcher for truth is to persevere in the process of weighing and comparing the input at his or her disposal. As for rational criteria and sensory data, these are the human instruments and measures that make such weighing and comparison possible for the purpose of arriving at the truth. If one has reason to believe that one's understanding of the revelation conflicts with human interests, one must search for greater understanding of either the revelation or the scientific facts of relevance to the issue at hand. In this way, one will be able to discern the course of action that is most in keeping with the spirit of the Islamic law even if it happens to differ from earlier rulings based on the text under consideration. However, what this approach tells us is not that there is more than one truth. Rather, it simply points to the differences that exist among situations, perspectives, and circumstances from one time or place to another. If understood properly, this insight does not create division; rather, it affirms that there is unity in diversity, and diversity in unity.

The Islamic Worldview Between the Prophet's Companions and the Desert Arabs

If, after the passing of the Prophet's Companions, the Muslim community had continued to adhere to the Qur'anic worldview – realizing the objective, integral connection that exists between revelation and nature – we would have preserved our unity as a nation; we would have led the way in the development of Islamic social sciences; and we would not have split up into warring factions and parties. In this event, it would not have been possible for the 'pharaoh' and 'priest' syndicates to mislead the public and destroy its unity – with either secular, liberal, and democratic slogans or religious platitudes, presenting falsehood and self-serving goals as disguises for a quest for truth and justice. Yet, in fact, all of these errors and crimes have been committed without regard for the genuine interests of the Muslim individual or community, and without regard for objective facts. Bogus personal choices and unproven axioms and hypotheses have been treated as though they were established facts, and in the process, truth and genuine human interests have been lost, the community has been torn apart, and its members have all but gone their separate ways.

If Islamic thought had continued to be governed by Qur'anic concepts and understandings, there would have been a realization that the words the Prophet spoke to the desert Arab tribes (that is, the Bedouin tribes) were tailored to their specific needs and capacities, and to the cultural and historical phase through which they were passing. As the Prophet himself once cautioned, "Speak to people in ways that they can understand."[4] And as Muslim quotes ʿAbd Allāh ibn Masʿūd as saying, "If you talk to people over their heads, your words are bound to become a source of temptation and trial to some of them." It appears, however, that this wisdom was not taken to heart by Muslim thinkers, who demonstrated a lack of awareness of the specific, time- and place-bound nature of the discourse the Prophet had addressed to the desert Arabs. Over time, this lack of awareness contributed to a willingness to accept much that – for innumerable reasons and motives – had been interpolated into Islamic writings by way of tribal, Jewish, Gnostic, and superstitious notions and traditions. This, in turn, led to a clouding of the Qur'anic worldview, which impeded the progress of Islamic civilization by putting a damper on its spirit, it dynamism, and its creative thought patterns. Over time, the Qur'an came to be thought of as little more than a means of acquiring a blessing and a heavenly reward through its recitation and memorization while, at the same time, there was little in the way of ijtihad (attempts to grapple with its meanings in new and creative ways). There came to be an exaggerated emphasis on writings that contained historical applications of Qur'anic teachings based on a purely linguistic understanding of the text, while the Muslim community fell prey increasingly to lethargy, stagnation, passivity, superstition, and sophistry. As a consequence, the foundation of knowledge and strength upon which this community had originally been founded began to crumble, while the guiding light of reflection, investigation, creativity, and conscious stewardship steadily died out.

The Bedouin Arabs' perspective – colored as it was by their exclusivist, dictatorial, chauvinistic tribal traditions and ways of thinking – had thus come to be a dominant force in the Muslim community. This development was reinforced by the entry into Islam of still other peoples, who brought with them traditions and notions inherited from their own autocratic cultures. Another factor at work, as we have seen, was the failure to distinguish carefully between the timeless, placeless discourse of the Qur'an and the practical Prophetic discourse that had been addressed specifically to the pagan Arabs of the Arabian peninsula in light of their particular circumstances. The focus of this applied discourse was on the fundamentals of the religion and the building of the community and society through ritual prayer and zakah. When the Prophet addressed the desert Arab tribes with the words, "Either submit to Islam, or be prepared for combat," his aim was to bring them out of their primitive social and cultural state into an understanding of the basic starting points for creating a global civilization based on the Qur'an and its teachings. However, this discourse of threat was, despite its time-and circumstance-bound nature, allowed to eclipse those teachings of the Qur'an that go beyond any one time, place, or circumstance and speak to human beings of all nations and ages.

All the aforementioned factors played a part in the distortion of the Islamic-Qur'anic vision that had guided the Prophet's Companions. With this distortion, moreover, increasing emphasis came to be given to a rhetoric of threat addressed to hostile, obdurate deniers of truth. This being the case, in the face of subsequent challenges and developments and against the background of the failure to distinguish between the believer who had mistakenly gone off track and the recalcitrant rebel – between the lost soul and the antagonistic, stubborn infidel – the way had been paved for further regression in the Muslim community on the levels of both thought and cultural achievement.

Consequently, it is important for us to distinguish here between the Qur'anic worldview of the Companions that had dazzled the world around them, and that of the primitive desert Arabs, which was reflected in what might be termed 'the minimalist discourse that the Prophet had addressed to them by virtue of his role as a wielder of authority in their society.' By telling them, in effect, "Either submit to Islam, or prepare for war," the Prophet's aim was to establish the basic structure of a civilized human society among these primitive pagan tribes in the simplest, least demanding of forms, and to do this by emphasizing the pillars of Islam, particularly those of prayer (with its cohesive force) and zakah (with its capacity to affirm and enhance social solidarity and cooperation). Needless to say, the two points of view stood worlds apart: the civilized Qur'anic worldview that the Prophet's Companions lived by and passed on, and the primitive worldview of the desert Arabs, together with the coarse rhetoric they were able to understand.

The Companions gathered around the Messenger of God to learn the Qur'an and its civilized, universal worldview. This worldview spans human history, from man's creation as God's vicegerent and steward on earth – "...Behold, I am about to establish upon earth one who shall inherit it" (*sūrah al-Baqarah*, 2:30) – until, when those who dwell thereon fulfill their purposes through the creative, beneficial use of the earth's resources: "...until, when the earth has assumed its artful adornment and has been embellished, and they who dwell on it believe that they have gained mastery over it - there comes down upon it Our judgment, by night or by day,..." (*sūrah Yūnus*, 10:24). The Companions, then, were students of the Holy Qur'an; when they had heard ten verses of it, they would stop, commit them to memory, then act on them under the watchful eye of God's Chosen One as the teacher, example, and guide whose character was reflected in the Qur'an:

> for behold, thou keepest indeed to a sublime way of life; (*sūrah al-Qalam*, 68:4)

> And [thus, O Prophet,] We have sent thee as [an evidence of Our] grace towards all the worlds. (*sūrah al-Anbiyā'*, 21:107)

It should come as no surprise, then, to find that when, in certain exceptional circumstances, someone would write down an action or a statement of the Prophet, he would instruct them to erase what they had written. It was for this reason that during the days of the Prophet and the rightly guided caliphs, hadiths – that is, reports concerning something the Messenger of God had said, done, or approved – were not recorded with the accuracy and precision with which the Qur'an was recorded. The reason for this is simply that the Qur'an, rather than the hadiths, is the source of the timeless, abiding Islamic worldview. At the same time, this is not inconsistent with the fact that the Messenger of God instructed his people to obey his commands and directions in view of his being their earthly authority and head of state. Indeed, no one was to refrain from obeying the Prophet's commands on the pretext that they were not found in the Qur'an, since the concrete, detailed applications which his commands represented were not part of the Qur'an's function. Rather, the Qur'an is a constitution, an eternal message, a call, a law, and a worldview whose validity spans all times and places:

> *Ṭā'. Sīn. Mīm.* These are messages of the divine writ, clear in itself and clearly showing the truth. (*sūrah al-Shuʿarā'*, 26:1–2)

> ...No single thing have We neglected in Our decree... (*sūrah al-Anʿām*, 6:38)

> *Alif. Lām. Rā'.* A divine writ [is this], with messages that have been made clear in and by themselves, and have been distinctly spelled out as well – [bestowed upon you] out of the grace of One who is wise, All-Aware,... (*sūrah Hūd*, 11:1)

> *Alif. Lām. Rā'.* A divine writ [is this – a revelation] which We have bestowed upon thee from on high in order that thou might bring forth all mankind, by their Sustainer's leave, out of the depths of darkness into the light:... (*sūrah Ibrāhīm*, 14:1)

> This [revelation, then,] is a means of insight for mankind, and a guidance

and grace unto people who are endowed with inner certainty. (*sūrah al-Jāthiyah*, 45:20)

The function of the Qur'an is not to issue instructions or promulgate laws pertaining to the management of society and its affairs in specific times and places; rather, its function is to set forth the timeless, divinely inspired worldview, which the Prophet so wisely applied in specific circumstances "O our Sustainer! Raise up from the midst of our offspring an apostle from among themselves, who shall convey unto them Thy messages, and impart unto them revelation as well as wisdom, and cause them to grow in purity: for, verily, Thou alone art Almighty, truly Wise!" (*sūrah al-Baqarah*, 2:129), and in light of whose concepts and principles such societal management was intended to take place throughout subsequent history. It is this fact which can help us to understand why, after certain Companions who had gone out to various cities and begun teaching people hadiths concerning the Prophet's words and actions, the rightly guided caliph ʿUmar ibn al-Khaṭṭāb issued instructions for them to return to Madinah, since people residing in these other cities, unlike the people of Madinah itself, would not be able to understand what the hadiths meant, the Prophet's purpose behind the actions he had taken, and the words he had spoken, or the circumstances out of which they had arisen.

A thorough study of the history of Islamic scholarship makes clear that tribal ways and thinking, together with the influx of non-Arab peoples into the Muslim community, exerted a major impact on the course of the Arab nation-state following the defeat of the heirs to the Madinah School, who were isolated from the Muslim community's public affairs and relegated instead to the realm of private worship and personal affairs. The forerunner of the Madinah School and the founder of the 'Opinion School' (*madrasat al-ra'y*) was Imam Abū Ḥanīfah al-Nuʿmān (d. 150/767), whose approach was founded upon the principles of reasoned opinion, reflection on the Qur'an, and the wisdom embodied in the Prophet's applications of Qur'anic teachings to specific situations. When arguing for this or that opinion or ruling, Imam Abū Ḥanīfah contented himself with minimal citations from the Prophetic Sunnah. However, this does not mean that the texts of the Sunnah and the wisdom embodied in its applications of

Qur'anic teachings were not present in the minds of Imam Abū Ḥanīfah and other adherents of his school of thought as they reflected and wrote. Like Abū Ḥanīfah, Imam Mālik ibn Anas (d. 179/795) included relatively few (five hundred) Prophet hadiths in his *Muwaṭṭa'*; moreover, if he encountered a conflict between the accounts found in the Sunnah and the views adopted by thinkers of the Madinah School, he would adopt the latter rather than the former – the reason being that for Imam Mālik in particular, the conclusions reached by thinkers of the Madinah School were most in keeping with the thought and practice that were prevalent in the days of the Prophet himself.

We see a contrast, however, in the case of Imam Aḥmad ibn Ḥanbal, the founder of the last of the four Sunnite schools of jurisprudence, who developed his thought in Iraq – that is, in an environment that was distinct in many ways from that of Madinah. Iraq, which had been the birthplace of a number of bygone civilizations, witnessed critical developments during the rise of the Abbasid caliphate following the defeat of the Barmakids (*al-barāmikah*),[5] the power struggle between al-Amīn and al-Ma'mūn,[6] and the shift in the balance of power in favor of the Turks during al-Muʿtaṣim's reign. Needless to say, such events served to distance Imam Aḥmad in particular from the society that had existed during the days of the Prophet and to which the Prophet's applications of Qur'anic teaching had been suited. Consequently, as a way of addressing the crisis of thought that had arisen in his day, Imam Aḥmad included in his *Musnad* approximately forty thousand hadith narratives, many of which are weak,[7] and which he had chosen from among hundreds of thousands of hadiths and other narratives with which he was familiar. This work of Imam Aḥmad contributed to the proliferation of hadiths compilations and encyclopedias whose purpose, alas, was not primarily as a resource for readers to benefit from the wisdom to be gleaned from the ways in which the Messenger of God had applied Qur'anic teachings, but rather as a means of establishing their sanctity so that – as imitation became increasingly entrenched as a substitute for independent reasoning and interpretation and the creative application of Qur'anic concepts to new situations – such texts could serve as a means of holding at bay the incoming philosophies, cultures, and Gnostic thought systems that had begun impacting the thought of Muslim philosophers and mystics, scholastic philosophical movements, and politically oriented Shiite thought.

As a result of the aforementioned developments, most Muslim scholars ended up focusing on matters relating to personal piety, or what came to be termed *modes of worship* (*ᶜibādāt*) – even though, for the well-intentioned Muslim, every action he or she undertakes, public or private, is a form of worship. Similarly, scholars immersed themselves in attention to personal status laws and regulations governing mundane transactions such as sales agreements and the like. As a consequence, no real time or energy remained for writing books dealing with the public sphere, that is, the management of government affairs and public interests. The only books that did touch on such themes restricted themselves to nebulous exhortations to justice. To make things worse, such books were dedicated to the wielders of dictatorial powers, who would never have heeded such exhortations to begin with. The near-complete loss of the Islamic worldview with its balanced emphasis on the public and private spheres resulted in an overreliance on the rhetoric of threat and intimidation based on the assumption that the Muslim population at large was destined to remain ignorant, their faith weak, and their rulers' predisposition one of evil and disobedience. This type of rhetoric and assumptions enabled those in positions of power to don robes of bogus sanctity, while adopting the role of despotic caretaker in relation to the Muslim community. This posture was epitomized by the Abbasid caliph al-Manṣūr (d. 159/775) in his claim to be 'God's vicegerent on earth.' Islamic discourse thus appeared to have become devoted to the aim of negating both the self and the mind by encouraging servile acquiescence to the authority of bigoted tyrants. In so doing, it demonstrated wanton disregard for the Muslim community's bona fide right to oversee its rulers, whose duty is to protect their subjects' interests and lend their approval to the decisions that grow out of joint consultations between ruler and ruled.

It was only natural that – in response to the rhetoric of self-negation, the pitiful intellectual condition in which the Muslim community now found itself, and the erosion of its Islamic worldview – this should lead to a backlash in the form of self-centeredness, individualism, racism, egotism, and an unhealthy passivity. Such was a far cry from true self-realization as individuals and as a nation. Hence, decisive action, mastery, creativity, reform, self-giving, and exertion gave way to indecision, fear, meekness, and servility.

In this connection, it is important to note that the way in which the Messenger of God addressed his Companions was marked consistently by love, esteem, respect, and recognition of their noble qualities, accomplishments, and contributions. As such, it was a far cry from a rhetoric of contempt, humiliation, or intimidation. It is this kind of communication that reflects the Qur'anic view of others and the world. As God Almighty declares, "...all honour belongs to God, and [thus] to His Apostle and those who believe [in God]: but of this the hypocrites are not aware" (*sūrah al-Munāfiqūn*, 63:8). It follows, therefore, that Muslims should always be addressed with esteem and respect.

What is the Qur'anic Worldview?

The Qur'anic worldview is an ethical, monotheistic, purposeful, positive perspective on the world and those in it which reflects the healthy, well-balanced human nature that God created within us. It follows of necessity, then, that it is a scientific, law-governed perspective that supports responsible stewardship of the earth and its riches. Such a worldview aims to create an awareness of the elements that go to make up sound human nature, since it is only through such an awareness that we will possess the guidance we need in order to achieve true self-realization on both the individual and communal levels. True self-realization entails the ability to respond in moderation to our various needs and impulses, while exploring the horizons of human existence in all of its creative spiritual dimensions:

> As for anyone – be it man or woman – who does righteous deeds, and is a believer withal–him shall We most certainly cause to live a good life; and most certainly shall We grant unto such as these their reward in accordance with the best that they ever did. (*sūrah al-Naḥl*, 16:97)

When a person is living in harmony with his or her God-given human nature, there is a desire and willingness both to sacrifice oneself in order to ward off aggression, defend the truth, preserve human dignity, and pursue legitimate pleasures in life (the Prophet said that "making love to one's spouse merits a reward from God as though it were an act of charity"). Hence, in the Islamic worldview, one receives a reward in both cases. Similarly, one receives a reward for striving to earn an honest living for oneself and those one supports financially, for making responsible use of the resources at one's disposal, and for pursuing understanding and knowledge, be it spiritual or mundane. After all, none of these activities aims to bring harm to anyone or anything; on the contrary, they are positive endeavors that help to fulfill the meaning of life and its God-given purposes.

A Muslim who has grasped the Qur'anic worldview will live in harmony with his or her God-given nature, which is essentially good. It follows, then, that such a person will love God – Who is perfection and supreme purity, truth, justice, mercy, and peace. Conversely, he is bound to hate evil, which is synonymous with harm, injustice, corruption, cruelty, and aggression. These qualities are abhorrent to God, who warns us against them; it is only natural, then, that a believing Muslim will abhor them as well.

The Qur'anic worldview that we as Muslims are called upon to instill in our children's minds and hearts is a vision of love, dignity, and peace. Its warp is the belief in God's oneness, and its woof is the pursuit of knowledge and the purification of one's mind and emotions. Those steeped in the Qur'anic worldview will be blessed with a love for God, and with God's love for them. Such individuals freely offer themselves in service to God, since it is their nature to love Him who is truth, justice, and mercy, and since there is no one else that so deserves to be loved, and His approval sought. This includes one's own parents or children and even oneself, since the self has neither existence nor meaning apart from the love of God. If a person with a sound spiritual and doctrinal orientation observes crookedness or a desire for evil within himself, he will know no rest until he has turned away from it. This is what it means to love God; it means to love perfection, purity, and goodness and not to approve of oneself if one goes astray and commits any kind of evil or injustice.

This is the meaning of the words of the Prophet: "None of you has truly believed until I have become dearer to him then his children, his parents, and all people."[8] The same message is conveyed by the following exchange between ʿUmar ibn al-Khaṭṭāb and the Messenger of God:

> Once, taking the Prophet's hand, ʿUmar said, "O Messenger of God, I swear you are dearer to me than everything but my own soul!" He replied, saying, "By the One who holds my soul in His hand, I tell you, [you will not have perfect faith] until I am dearer to you than your own soul." "Therefore," replied ʿUmar, "you are now dearer to me than my own soul." "And now, O ʿUmar, [your faith has been perfected]!"[9]

What this tells us is that our faith will only be complete when we have become utterly sincere in our love for God, a love expressed in a pure, passionate love for goodness and truth in this world. It should also be remembered that love for the Prophet is part of love for God – since through his morals, his character, and his behavior, the Prophet served as the supreme human expression of what love for God means. As God Almighty once said to him, "– for behold, thou keepest indeed to a sublime way of life;" (*sūrah al-Qalam*, 68:4). Similarly, God declared to the early Muslim community:

> Indeed, there has come unto you [O mankind] an Apostle from among yourselves: heavily weighs upon him [the thought] that you might suffer [in the life to come]; full of concern for you [is he, and] full of compassion and mercy towards the believers. (*sūrah al-Tawbah*, 9:128)

And:

> Whoever pays heed unto the Apostle pays heed unto God thereby;... (*sūrah al-Nisā'*, 4:80)

Saʿd ibn Hishām relates that he once said to ʿĀ'ishah, "Tell me about the character of the Messenger of God," to which she replied, "His character was the Qur'an."[10] In sum, then, those who are sincere in their love for God and His attributes will also love His Messenger and what his attributes represent; they will also love in themselves whatever is consistent with these attributes, and will hate in themselves whatever comes in conflict with them.

Love for the Messenger of God and the members of his household with whom he has lived on intimate terms – including his wives, his daughters, his grandchildren and other relatives, as well as the Companions who believed in his message, followed him, learned from him, and were sincere in their faith and their struggle on behalf of the truth – is by no means a personality cult. Rather, it is a love for the noble qualities, values, and principles which he embodied; anything other than this is a departure from the sound path and a fall into the trap of racism, bigotry, and obsession with lineage that marred the Muslim community's Qur'anic vision in later days – thereby ossifying its social and institutional structures, facilitating tyranny and corruption, undermining its sense of solidarity as a nation, and contributing to the disintegration of Islamic civilization.

Given the centrality of Muslim's feelings toward God, particularly in the wake of the negative intellectual and cultural influences at work in modern-day materialistic culture, it is important to undertake socio-psychological studies that reflect the Qur'anic worldview and the centrality of love for God as the Most Compassionate, Loving, Generous One who is worthy of all praise and who turns to us in His mercy when we turn to Him in repentance. Such studies might take the form of literature dealing with parental and school-based educational materials emphasizing God's love for the Muslim child. In addressing adult audiences, attention should be given to conscious reflection on God's blessings and providential care and the ways in which He has honored human beings (" for although you see Him not, He sees you" – cited in Muslim). Anas ibn Mālik reports that the Messenger of God once said:

> God's joy over a servant of His who repents might be likened to that of a traveler who was passing through a barren, uninhabited expanse when suddenly, his mount broke away from him carrying all his food and drink. Despairing of ever seeing his mount again, the traveler betook himself to a nearby tree and went to sleep in its shade. When he awakened from his slumber, what should he find but his mount standing before him. Seeing his returned mount, he grasped it by the halter and, beside himself with joyous relief, cried, "O God, You art my servant, and I am thy Lord!" So intense was his joy, he failed to express himself coherently.[11]

Muslims need to be aware of the fact that love for God and the remembrance and worship of Him are only real if they bear fruit in the individual's life by, for example, his carrying out the tasks involved in responsible stewardship of the earth in a conscientious, creative manner. Otherwise, we show ourselves to be inferior to animals, plants, and inanimate objects, all of which praise God in their respective ways by behaving in conformity with the functions He has assigned them:

> ...and there is not a single thing but extols His limitless glory and praise: but you [O men] fail to grasp the manner of their glorifying Him! (*sūrah al-Isrā'*, 17:44)

> Art thou not aware that it is God whose limitless glory all [creatures] that are in the heavens and on earth extol, even the birds as they spread out their wings? Each [of them] know indeed how to pray unto Him and to glorify Him; and God has full knowledge of all that they do: (*sūrah al-Nūr*, 24:41)

> ...and be constant in prayer: for, behold, prayer restrains [man] from loathsome deeds and from all that runs counter to reason; and remembrance of God is indeed the greatest [good]. And God knows all that you do. (*sūrah al-ʿAnkabūt*, 29:45)

Abū Hurayrah reports that the Messenger of God once said, "Many a person who fasts gains nothing through his fasting but hunger, and many a person who spends the night in prayer has nothing to show for it but hours of sleep lost."[12] In this connection, Anas ibn Mālik related the following account:

> Three men once came to the houses of the Prophet's wives inquiring about the Prophet's devotional practices. When they had received answers to their questions, they replied – as though they were surprised to find that he was not more rigorous in his disciplines – "But how could we compare to the Prophet, whose past and future transgressions have all been forgiven?" (*sūrah al-Fath*, 48:2). One of them then said, "As for me, I spend every night in prayer." Another said, "I fast all year round." And the last of them added, "I abstain from all contact with women, and have never married." The Messenger of God then came and said, "Are you the ones who said such-and-such? God is my witness that I am the most

> God-fearing amongst you and the most conscious of Him. Nevertheless, I fast [at times] and break my fast [at others], I perform the ritual prayers [at times] and take my rest [at others], and I take women in marriage. And whoever spurns my example, has nothing to do with me."[13]

In a similar vein, ʿAbd Allāh ibn ʿAmrū ibn al-ʿĀṣ related the following encounter with the Prophet, saying, "The Messenger of God once asked me, "ʿAbd Allāh, is it true what I have been told, that you fast by day and pray by night?"'That is true, O Messenger of God,' I replied. 'Do it no longer,' he said to me. 'Rather, fast on some days, but not on others. Spend part of the night in prayer, but not all of it. For your body has rights over you, your eyes have rights over you, and likewise, your wife.'"[14]

Given what has been said thus far, we can begin to envision the implications of the Qur'anic worldview for our societal institutions by applying Qur'anic concepts to various areas of life. We can begin with the concepts of mutual consultation, justice, charity, the doing of good, and purification – as well as the opposing concepts of injustice, wrongdoing, aggression, and all that runs counter to reason and human interests. In so doing, we challenge the superficial view of the Qur'an as a book that is useful for nothing but recitation for the sake of receiving personal blessing and reward. In place of this view, we seek to establish a proper understanding of the Qur'an as the source of guidance and a constructive spiritual worldview on which to base our lives and our society. The Qur'an serves as a measuring rod for all our proposed aims and purposes – as well as a set of criteria on the basis of which to evaluate the content of narratives and other texts and their various interpretations so that that which conforms to Qur'anic criteria is judged to be valid, while that which violates them can be modified, set aside, or corrected.

A number of intellectual and cultural battles are currently raging due to the efforts of some to obliterate or marginalize Muslim identity and culture with its distinctive features and destroy its ability to make creative, reformative contributions to modern materialistic culture, whose deviations and distortions threaten human society and existence. An example of the issues around which such battles rage is that of women's rights and roles in the family and society. The institution of the family has historically been given special attention by Muslim scholars due to its vital connection to Islamic law. Consequently, the Muslim family has preserved its importance and moral strength despite the devastating atrophy and stagnation that has afflicted Islamic thought in the past. Hence, it is the Muslim family that has stood fast in the face of the storms of corruption that have wreaked such havoc on Muslim political life and led to the disintegration of Muslim society's public institutions.

Unless we reform the family and work systems in a manner that reflects the wisdom of creation manifested in men's and women's complementarity roles and responsibilities within the family structure, we will contribute even further to the destruction and disintegration of the Muslim community and its peoples. And in this event, it will be even more difficult for Muslim societies to rebuild their foundations and their hopes of contributing to the progress and well-being of contemporary human civilization.

When viewed from the perspective of the Qur'anic worldview, the relationship between the man and the woman is one of complementarity, not similarity. The complementary unity of the sexes brings harmony to human existence and to the physical, psychological, and social makeup of both the man and the woman, as a result of which the two of them together form a complete, synchronized entity. As we are reminded by the words of the Holy Qur'an:

> It is He who has created you [all] out of one living entity, and out of it brought into being its mate, so that man might incline [with love] towards woman.... (*sūrah al-Aʿrāf*, 7:189)

> And among His wonders is this: He creates for you mates out of your own kind, so that you might incline towards them, and He engenders love and tenderness between you: in this, behold, there are messages indeed for people who think! (*sūrah al-Rūm*, 30:21)

Hence, although the notion of male-female similarity that prevails in contemporary materialistic society claims to be based on an objective, scientific worldview, it nevertheless flies in the face of reality, and works at cross-purposes with our God-given human nature. Guided by little more than animal-like whims and impulses, this modern-day notion of the male-female dynamic demonstrates an arbitrary disregard for human nature as it really is and the laws of the cosmos that govern the psychological and physical dimensions of the relationship between male and female. Hence, rather than basing our thinking and behavior on the assumption that men and women are essentially alike, we as Muslims are to operate on the assumption that, while they may be alike in some respects, men and women are nevertheless distinct from one other in complementary ways.

The confusion that marks contemporary materialistic civilization with respect to the woman and the family is a glaring example of the coarse, perverted nature of the worldview on which this civilization is based. The materialistic worldview disregards or underplays the essential, organic psychological and social differences between men and women. We are witnessing the devastating effects of this view on Western societies, where this nihilistic, unwarranted, unscientific view has led to injustices against women and their dignity as well as against the rights of children, thereby destroying the institution of the family with its constructive ethical foundations.

Consequently, we should not be surprised at the turmoil and perversion that have resulted from the disintegration of the family and its morals in Western society. Given the distorted view that prevails of relations between women and men in the construction and development of human society, women have had to bear burdens that prevent them from fulfilling their motherly instincts – or, when they have chosen to fulfill this instinct, to bear alone the material and psychological costs of this choice. Meanwhile, men have been exempted from responsibility and been allowed to give free rein to their selfish inclinations, in some cases as brazen buffoons who spend their free time in nightclubs and brothels. At the same time, children have been deprived of fatherly nurture while women have, practically speaking, ceased to be viewed as mothers, wives, and daughters, being treated instead as chattels or commodities whose purpose is to provide passing satisfaction for men's whims and desires.

Unfortunately, lack of awareness of the Qur'anic worldview, its social dimensions and the structure of its cultural system, has served the interests of those engaged in the cultural dispossession of the Muslim community. Their task has been further facilitated by widespread infatuation with modern Western civilization's scientific and material achievements and the influence of the weapons and strategies employed in the service of such cultural invasion, including the use of artfully woven entertainment programs broadcast over satellite channels and Internet websites. Add to this, the Muslim community's lack of well-guided doctrinal, intellectual and educational tools of resistance, the weakness and superficiality of the Muslim intellectual and educational movement, and the dearth of authentic studies dealing with the Muslim personality and its circumstances in all of their positive and negative aspects in the diverse lands where Muslims reside.

The concept of monotheism and the purposeful, ethical view to which it gives rise lead in turn to the concept of complementarity. The concept of complementarity provides a positive explanation of the similarities and differences that exist between men and women. Similarly, it provides a means of ordering social relationships between men and women and their resulting rights and responsibilities in light of their God-given natures and the Qur'anic concepts of love (*al-mawaddah*), compassion (*al-raḥmah*), the doing of good (*al-maʿrūf*), and charity (*al-iḥsān*). As a result, every party to this human relationship is able to achieve self-realization in the best, most positive sense of the word, enjoy fair treatment, and receive assistance in performing his or her role in the variety of situations, areas, and phases that life entails.

Our understanding of the Qur'anic worldview continues to be murky as it relates to modern Islamic thought, while Islamic thought – based solely on traditional models, particularly with respect to family relationships and laws established in earlier historical periods and in locations other than our own – is ineffective and inflexible. Consequently, there is a need for a more thorough understanding of the Qur'anic worldview and its associated concepts. Moreover, this worldview needs to be understood on a deeper level not only as it relates to the marital relationship between the man and the woman, but in addition, as it relates to the kind of practical reformulation that guarantees the rights of both the man and the woman in the economic, political, social, and educational domains. Such a reformulation will make it possible for these spheres to begin operating harmoniously in keeping with Qur'anic concepts and principles, thereby forming integrated subsystems within the broader system represented by society as a whole. When this takes places, both spouses will become better able to perform their respective functions and tasks and the woman will receive fairer treatment, particularly during the phases of her greatest vulnerability, namely, those of pregnancy, lactation and childrearing, since the task of motherhood belongs to the woman in particular, and no one but she can perform it.

In light of the Islamic worldview and Qur'anic concepts and values, this, then, is one example of the issues that modern-day Islamic thought needs to grapple with in a progressive, forceful manner. It is also important for us to observe that the community or nation in the Qur'anic worldview is understood to be an inseparable part of human existence, which is only complete when the life of the individual is complemented by that of the community. For, in fact, the individual has no real existence apart from the collectivity to which he or she belongs, just as the community has no existence apart from the individuals that make it up. Similarly, the individual's well-being and prosperity depend on the strength of the community and the soundness of its structure, just as the strength and prosperity of the community depend on the degree to which its members master their work, their sincerity and dedication, their participation, and their willing contributions. Hence, the discourse of the Qur'an is addressed to the individual, to the community, and to the human race as a whole:

> God has promised those of you who have attained to faith and do righteous deeds that, of a certainty, He will cause them to accede to power on earth. (*sūrah al-Nūr*, 24:55)

> And say [unto them, O Prophet]: "Act! And God will behold your deeds, and [so will] His Apostle, and the believers:..." (*sūrah al-Tawbah*, 9:105)

> O Mankind! Worship your Sustainer, who has created you and those who lived before you, so that you might remain conscious of Him. (*sūrah al-Baqara*, 2:21)

The aforementioned verses point to three foundations for successful human action according to the Qur'anic worldview, namely: (1) the strength of one's certainty and faith, (2) the productivity of one's action, and (3) the effectiveness of one's action due to its righteousness. The effectiveness and productivity of one's action are related to one's adherence to a scientific objectivity in one's approach, or what has been traditionally termed *rightness* (*al-ṣalāḥ*). Hence, someone who fails to perceive the facts and laws of the cosmos as they are in relation to what he does will receive a single reward in the afterlife, namely, the reward for faith and good intentions –whereas someone who perceives them correctly in relation to what he does will receive two rewards, namely, the reward for faith and good intentions, and the reward for outward rightness or usefulness (*al-ṣalāḥ*). If, for example, someone wishes to dig a well but does not understand the objective facts pertaining to how and where to dig it, he will be rewarded in the afterlife for his good intention; as for someone who not only wishes to dig a well but, in addition, understands how and where to dig it, he will receive both a reward in the afterlife for his intention to dig it, and the earthly reward of having actually been able to obtain cold water.

If the Muslim community, collectively and individually, wishes to release its dormant psychological and spiritual energy, its members have no choice but to reflect on the Qur'anic worldview, then labor to recapture its values and concepts as they apply to belief, emotions, and their perceptions of the environment and the meaning of existence. Well did ʿUmar ibn al-Khaṭṭāb speak when, in giving voice to the clear-sighted, Qur'an-inspired, responsible, realistic approach to life by which he and the other Companions of the Prophet lived, he said, "I flee from the decree of God (His laws and statutes) to the decree of God (His laws and statutes)."[15]

Self and Other in the Qur'anic Worldview

If this is the kind of dynamism and guidance which the Qur'anic worldview offers the Muslim community, then what does it have to offer to others? And who are these 'others'? What governs the relationship between Self and Other in the Qur'anic view of the world? The path before us will only be clear when we have clarified this vital human dimension of the Qur'anic perspective on the world and human life. Given the universal, integrative dimension of the Qur'an's monotheistic vision, the 'Other' is seen to be an integral part of the 'I,' just as the 'I' is understood to be an integral part of the 'Other.' When seen from the perspective of the Qur'anic worldview, relationships between this or that Self and this or that Other are viewed as interpenetrating circles – each of which has something beneficial to contribute to the other, and which together form an exquisite tapestry of purposefulness, integration, coordination, and constructive interaction. It is in this kind of a context – that is, in one ruled by the ideals of justice, tolerance, brotherhood, and peace – that the meaning of individual and collective human existence is fulfilled.

Self and Other in the Qur'anic worldview – male or female, black or white, believer or non-believer – are all equally members of the human race, brought together and united by the fact of their belonging to the human totality. Seen from the Qur'anic perspective, all human beings are a single entity, created equally as brothers and sisters and members of the greater human family:

> O mankind! Be conscious of your Sustainer, who has created you out of one living entity, and out of it created its mate, and out of the two spread abroad a multitude of men and women. And remain conscious of God, in whose name you demand [your rights] from one another, and of these ties of kinship. Verily, God is ever watchful over you!... (*sūrah al-Nisā'*, 4:1)

Self and Other in the Qur'anic discourse – men and women, derived from a single soul – have been granted diverse and separate existences in order to complete one another as mates, peoples, and nations who are brought and held together by the bonds of loving-kindness and compassion.

Self and Other are people who belong to 'peoples and tribes' in a variety of human social systems which, despite their underlying unity, represent diversity. By virtue of this diversity there can be shared interaction, knowledge of one another, and integration. If all parts were identical there could be no interaction or complementarity. Attraction, for example, does not take place between two positive or two negative poles, but only between a positive pole and a negative one. Interaction, like attraction, requires cooperation and complementarity; it is for this reason that human beings were created to branch out as diverse peoples and tribes – as males and females, with varying abilities and capacities, so that they could interact, come to know one another, and help bring one another to completion:

> ...[He] brought you into being out of the earth, and made you thrive thereon.... (*sūrah Hūd*, 11:61)

> For, He it is who has made you inherit the earth, and has raised some of you by degrees above others, so that He might try you by means of what He has bestowed upon you.... (*sūrah al-Anʿām*, 6:165)

Hence, difference and diversity in the Qur'anic worldview have nothing to do with racism or one group's or individual's being superior to another; rather, they have to do with unity and a supportive human complementarity, which is vital to the existence of both the individual and the community.

Self and Other differ in terms of 'tongues and colors' through which creativity and beauty manifest themselves in the creation from the level of the individual to that of tribes, peoples, and races. On the level of their human essence, however, "no Arab is superior to a non-Arab, nor white to black, unless it be by virtue of God-consciousness." (the Prophet's last sermon):

> And among His wonders is the creation of the heavens and the earth, and the diversity of your tongues and colours: for in this, behold, there are messages indeed for all who are possessed of [innate] knowledge! (*sūrah al-Rūm*, 30:22)

Qur'anically speaking, Self and Other exist on all levels: the individual, the communal, the global. They may be related by marriage or by blood; they may be neighbors; they may be fellow citizens of the world from across the globe. In all cases, however, such relationships can be likened to concentric and interpenetrating circles held together through justice, peace, good will, compassion, tolerance, cooperation, and mutual support:

> And among His wonders is this: He creates for you mates out of your own kind, so that you might incline towards them, and He engenders love and

tenderness between you: in this, behold, there are messages indeed for people who think! (*sūrah al-Rūm*, 30:21)

> And give his due to the near of kin, as well as to the needy and the wayfarer, but do not squander [thy substance] senselessly. (*sūrah al-Isrā'*, 17:26)

> ...You shall worship none but God; and you shall do good unto your parents and kinsfolk, and the orphans, and the poor; and you shall speak unto all people in a kindly way; and you shall be constant in prayer; and you shall spend in charity. (*sūrah al-Baqarah*, 2:83)

Self and Other differ from one another in terms of abilities and potentials "...to the end that they might avail themselves of one another's help...," (*sūrah al-Zukhruf*, 43:32). Such differences and distinctions exist not in order for one person or group to lord it over another or to think of himself as superior to others; rather, they exist in order for people to cooperate and to complement each other in united endeavors to make responsible use of the planet and its resources, to provide for their own and others' needs, and to produce civilizations and cultures. Hence, differences and distinctions within the human community are a blessing, indeed, a necessity, for without them no one of us – whatever his or her race, color, language, or abilities – would survive:

> ...but rather help one another in furthering virtue and God-consciousness, and do not help one another in furthering evil and enmity; and remain conscious of God: for, behold, God is severe in retribution! (*sūrah al-Mā'idah*, 5:2)

> O you who have attained to faith! No men shall deride [other] men: it may well be that those [whom they deride] are better than themselves; and no women [shall deride other] women: it may well be that those [whom they deride] are better than themselves. And neither shall you defame one another, nor insult one another by [opprobrious] epithets: evil is all imputation of iniquity after [one has attained to] faith, and they who [become guilty thereof and] do not repent – it is they, they who are evildoers! (*sūrah al-Ḥujurāt*, 49:11)

We are called upon in the Qur'an to exhort others to do good in a spirit of gentleness, earnestness, and kindness: "help one another in furthering virtue and God-consciousness" (*sūrah al- Mā'idah*, 5:2). We are to seek always to guide each other with words of wisdom, encourage others to do good, and discourage them from doing what is harmful or contrary to reason and prudence:

> Call thou [all mankind] unto thy Sustainer's path with wisdom and goodly exhortation, and argue with them in the most kindly manner:... (*sūrah al-Naḥl*, 16:125)

> And [thus it is:] had thy Sustainer so willed, all those who live on earth would surely have attained to faith, all of them: dost thou, then, think that thou couldst compel people to believe. (*sūrah Yūnus*, 10:99)

> You are indeed the best community that has ever been brought forth for [the good of] mankind: you enjoin the doing of what is right and forbid the doing of what is wrong, and you believe in God.... (*sūrah Āl ʿImrān*, 3:110)

The Messenger of God said, "If someone goes into combat out of blind allegiance to this or that group or blind hostility against this or that group and is killed in battle, he meets his death at the hands of ignorance."[16]

Self and Other differ in attitudes and perspectives; this simply reflects the nature of creation, which is characterized by diversity in unity, and unity in diversity. Hence, the Other, in whatever ways he or she differs from the Muslim, is worthy of all respect on both the spiritual and material levels, and the relationship between them is to be one of tolerance, kindness, fairness, and justice:

> As for such [of the unbelievers] as do not fight against you on account of [your] faith, and neither drive you forth from your homelands, God does not forbid you to show them kindness and to behave towards them with full equity: for, verily, God loves those who act equitably. (*sūrah al-Mumtaḥinah*, 60:8)

By virtue of their unity as human beings and the mutual belonging this entails, it is justice alone which must govern the relationship between Self and Other even in situations in which there is enmity and alienation. For without justice, neither the bond of humanity nor the responsibility to act as stewards of the creation has any meaning:

> O you who have attained to faith! Be ever steadfast in your devotion to God, bearing witness to the truth in all equity; and never let hatred of anyone lead you into the sin of deviating from justice. Be just: this is closest to being God-conscious. And remain conscious of God: verily, God is aware of all that you do. (*sūrah al-Mā'idah*, 5:8)

Similarly, the brotherly bond born of their common humanity requires that Self and Other avoid all injustice and aggression toward one another. Even when repelling aggression and defending those wronged or oppressed, there is no justification for hostilities beyond what is required to put a stop to the other's aggression and to whatever injustice is being perpetrated. Rather, it is preferable to pardon whenever possible:

> And fight in God's cause against those who wage war against you, but do not commit aggression – for, verily, God does not love aggressors. (*sūrah al-Baqarah*, 2:190)

> ...help one another in furthering virtue and God-consciousness, and do not help one another in furthering evil and enmity;... (*sūrah al-Mā'idah*, 5:2)

> But whoever deliberately slays another believer, his requital shall be hell, therein to abide; and God will condemn him, and will reject him, and will prepare for him awesome suffering. (*sūrah al-Nisā'*, 4:93)

It is not without reason that the Qur'an refers to the act of repelling aggression as itself aggression: "Thus, if anyone commits aggression against you, attack him just as he has attacked you" (*fa man iᶜtadā ᶜalaykum faᶜtadū ᶜalayhi bi mithli mā iᶜtadā ᶜalaykum*).[17] The reason for this Qur'anic appellation is that conflict and warfare among brothers in humanity always, and inevitably, involves the crossing of a red line of sorts. Hence, even the legitimate right to repel another's act of aggression (*radd al-ᶜudwān*) when necessary is referred to as aggression (*al-ᶜudwān*). In this way, the Qur'an alerts us to the seriousness of such an action, as well as to the dignity and value of human life. In keeping with this message, we are admonished concerning the need to be conscious of God and to fear Him in all that we do. As Abel once replied to Cain, "Even if thou lay thy hand on me to slay me, I shall not lay my hand on thee to slay thee; behold, I fear God, the Sustainer of all the worlds" (*sūrah al-Mā'idah*, 5:28).

The Muslim is always both just and moderate, seeking to be equitable in all he does and allowing all his conduct, toward himself and toward others, to be governed by the values and purposes that are in keeping with justice and moderation. Without moderation there can be no justice; indeed, justice is simply a fruit of moderation in all things – in tranquility and in anger, in giving and in receiving. In times of peace, moderation yields brotherhood and harmony, and when repelling aggression, it leads one to act with both strength and generosity of spirit:

> O you who have attained to faith! Be ever steadfast in upholding equity, bearing witness to the truth for the sake of God, even though it be against your own selves or your parents and kinsfolk.... (*sūrah al-Nisā'*, 4:135)

> ...and never let hatred of anyone lead you into the sin of deviating from justice. Be just: this is closest to being God-conscious. And remain conscious of God: verily, God is aware of all that you do. (*sūrah al-Mā'idah*, 5:8)

> ...and has laid no hardship on you in [anything that pertains to] religion,... (*sūrah al-Ḥajj*, 22:78)

> God does not burden any human being with more than he is well able to bear: in his favor shall be whatever good he does, and against him whatever evil he does. "O our Sustainer! Take us not to task if we forget or unwittingly do wrong!..." (*sūrah al-Baqarah*, 2:286)

> And give his due to the near of kin, as well as to the needy and the wayfarer, but do not squander [thy substance] senselessly. Behold, the squanderers are, indeed, of the ilk of the satans – inasmuch as Satan has indeed proved most ungrateful to his Sustainer. (*sūrah al-Isrā'*, 17:26–27)

> And thus have We willed you to be a community of the middle way, so that [with your lives] you might bear witness to the truth before all mankind, and that the Apostle might bear witness to it before you.... (*sūrah al-Baqarah*, 2: 143)

In a *ḥadīth qudsī*[18] transmitted by Abū Dharr on the authority of the Prophet, God states, "O My servants, I have forbidden injustice to myself and have likewise rendered it forbidden among you. Therefore, commit no injustice against one another."[19] In the account of the farewell address delivered by the Prophet during his final pilgrimage to Makkah, ʿAbd Allāh ibn ʿUmar states:

> We were discussing the Farewell Pilgrimage once with the Messenger of God in our midst. At that time, we did not yet know what the Farewell Pilgrimage was. The Messenger of God then uttered praise to God and said, "God has rendered your lives and your property as sacred as this day of yours, in this land of yours, in this month of yours. Do you hear what I am saying?" "We hear you," his listeners replied. He then continued, saying, "O God, bear witness!"[20]

In the same vein, Ḥudhayfah relates that the Messenger of God said: "Do not be double-minded people who say, 'If others are good to us, we will be good to them, and if others wrong us, we will wrong them. Rather, accustom yourselves to doing good to others whether they do good to you or not.'"[21] The Prophet's wife ʿĀ'ishah reported having heard the Messenger of God say, "Anything, if accompanied by kindness, is beautified thereby, and anything, if lacking in kindness, is thereby abased."[22]

Both the Other and the I are integral parts of the individual, since the human personality is far from simple; on the contrary, it is a highly complex entity. It includes, for example, both the self that "incite[s] to evil" (*al-nafs al-ammārah bi al-sū'*) (*sūrah Yūsuf*, 12:53) and "the accusing voice of man's own conscience" (*al-nafs al-lawwāmah*) (*sūrah al-Qiyāmah*, 75:2). As such, it is an entity with multiple associations, allegiances, and extensions, and it comprises dimensions that are both indispensable and inseparable from the individual, from humanity (since the 'I' is the human being, and humanity is an inseparable part of the 'I') to the clan, tribe and nation, to neighbors and blood relations.

In seeking to meet their needs, both Self and Other should bear in mind that within each one of us, complex beings that we are, there are both base and aggressive impulses ruled by the 'law of the jungle' where 'might is right' (the self that incites to evil, *al-nafs al-ammārah bi al-sū'*), and spiritual, altruistic aspirations that lead us to strive for fairness, compassion, and peace. Such aspirations, which are governed by the law of justice where 'right is might' – that is to say, where power and strength are derived from truth – cause human beings to incline toward values of truth and justice and to resist impulses that are hedonistic, aggressive, and racist.

When Self and Other are both Muslims, they are joined by a common identity based on doctrine, belief, and vision, which lie at the heart of what it means to be a human being. After all, the essence of human existence is not forms, appearances, or the merely physical – however important these may be as resources and tools for carrying out our various tasks and giving expression to the content of our visions, values, and principles, and despite the fact that human beings would have no existence without material reality and its practical, creative, and aesthetic manifestations. Hence, the brotherhood that exists between Muslims is more precious than that which is based on our common humanity alone, since shared belief helps to form the most powerful spiritual bond on earth:

> All believers are but brethren.... (*sūrah al-Ḥujurāt*, 49:10)

> O you who have attained to faith! Be conscious of God with all the consciousness that is due to Him, and do not allow death to overtake you ere you have surrendered yourselves unto Him. And hold fast, all together, unto the bond with God, and do not draw apart from one another. And remember the blessings which God has bestowed upon you: how, when you were enemies, He brought your hearts together, so that through His blessing you became brethren;... (*sūrah Āl ͨImrān*, 3:102–103)

> And [as for] the believers, both men and women – they are close unto one another: they [all] enjoin the doing of what is right and forbid the doing of what is wrong, and are constant in prayer, and render the purifying dues, and pay heed unto God and His Apostle. It is they upon whom God will bestow His grace: verily, God is Almighty, Wise! (*sūrah al-Tawbah*, 9:71)

ͨAbd Allāh ibn ͨUmar reports that the Prophet said, "The Muslim is a brother to his fellow Muslim. Hence, he should never wrong him or abandon him."[23] ͨAbd Allāh ibn ͨUmar also related that the Prophet said, "The true Muslim is someone from whose words and actions other Muslims have no reason to fear harm, while the true Emigrant is someone who has abandoned all that God has forbidden."[24] Abū Mūsā al-Ashʿarī relates that the Messenger of God once said, "One believer is to another as one stone is to another in a mighty edifice, each of them serving to support the other and hold it in place."[25] He also said, "So great is the compassion, affection, and sympathy shared by the believers that they are like a single body: if any member of the body suffers, all other parts of the body call out to one another with wakefulness and fever."[26] Similarly, he commanded, "Desire for your brother what you desire for yourself."[27] And in his farewell address, he reminded the Muslims with him of the sacred bond among them, saying, "O people! Your lives and your property are to be treated with the same sanctity as this day of yours, in this land of yours, in this month of yours until the Day on which you meet your Lord. Do you hear what I am saying?" "We hear you," his listeners replied. He then continued, saying, "O God, have I delivered the message?"[28] The Prophet's wife ʿĀ'ishah related that he had said, "Anyone who goes to bed on a full stomach knowing that his neighbor is hungry is not a believer."[29] Abū Hurayrah reported that the Messenger of God had said, "God will come to the aid of the servant who comes to the aid of his brother,"[30] and, "Everything associated with the Muslim – his life, his honor, and his possessions – is to be viewed by his fellow Muslims as sacred."[31] Abū Saʿīd al-Khudrī related that the Messenger of God had said, "You have a single Lord and a single forefather. Therefore, the Arab is not superior to the non-Arab, nor the non-Arab to the Arab, nor the red-skinned to the black-skinned, nor the black-skinned to the red-skinned, except on the basis of greater consciousness of God."[32] Anas related that the Messenger of God had said, "Come to the aid of your brother whether he has been wronged or has done wrong to another." Hearing what the Prophet had said, one man said, "O Messenger of God, I will gladly come to my brother's aid if he has been wronged. But how can I do so if he has wronged someone else?" The Prophet replied, "You come to his aid by restraining him or preventing him from doing [further] wrong."[33] Ḥudhayfah related that the Messenger of God had said, "Whoever does not show concern for the Muslims as a community does not belong to them."[34]

The brotherhood of Islam is thus a brotherhood founded upon goodness, truth, justice, righteousness, kindness, and compassion. It is a brotherhood of solidarity and cooperation in the doing of good and the fear of God. Consequently, it is the sublimest, most powerful possible expression of human belonging. If Muslims realized the implications of this type of belonging and brotherhood for today's world, and if they truly assimilated the Qur'anic worldview, they would truly be a single nation, a united family, a guiding light, and a constructive, creative force.

In the Qur'anic worldview, Self and Other represent diverse associations and affiliations all of which are 'I,' since one's identity is comprised of links to others based on blood, marriage, race, and humanity, as well as doctrine and thought. At the same time, it is a single entity composed of all these associations, every one of which renders the 'I' a 'they' as well, and the 'they' an 'I.'

Consequently, the trust embodied in the duty of stewardship requires that the Muslim take on constructive, reformist inclinations and values. If the honest Muslim is remiss in any of his responsibilities toward himself or others, he will repent and correct himself. Faithfulness to the task of being a good steward of God's gifts calls for the acquisition and cultivation of personal character traits that enable us to translate our God-given responsibilities into realities in our behavior and our relationships. The Qur'an has detailed such character traits for us; hence, if a Muslim discovers that he lacks these qualities in himself and that, as a consequence, they are not reflected in his actions and his relationships with others, be they human beings, animals, or other aspects of his environment, then he needs to examine himself, hold himself accountable, and strive to cultivate those virtues that will enable him to take on the God-given trust, which constitutes the meaning of his life – and his response to which will determine his destiny.

Carrying out one's God-given responsibilities requires, first of all, honesty, faithfulness to one's word, a spirit of fairness, a refusal to engage in wrongdoing or aggression, humility, charity, and generosity toward others, and a commitment to act with integrity and shun corruption. If a Muslim finds that he has a tendency to be harsh, cruel, or violent, to be wasteful or extravagant in his spending, to lie, to break promises and not to live up to responsibilities or commitments he has taken on, then he should be aware that his faith and worship are lacking. In response to this awareness, he must face himself, recognize his error, and turn away from it before that Day when "...neither wealth will be of any use, nor children, [and when] only he [will be happy] who comes before God with a heart free of evil!" (*sūrah al-Shuʿarā'*, 26:88–89). It is clear from both the Qur'an and the life of the Messenger of God that if one lacks the above-mentioned virtues, his faith is not genuine, nor has he benefited from the acts of devotion he engages in – be they prayer, remembrance of the Divine Name, fasting, or spending the night hours in prayer and worship:

> ...And be true to every promise – for, verily, [on Judgment Day] you will be called to account for every promise which you have made! (*sūrah al-Isrā'*, 17:34)

> Hence, O my people, [always] give full measure and weight, with equity, and do not deprive people of what is rightfully theirs, and do not act wickedly on earth by spreading corruption. (*sūrah Hūd*, 11:85)

> And neither allow thy hand to remain shackled to thy neck, nor stretch it forth to the utmost limit [of thy capacity], lest thou find thyself blamed [by thy dependants], or even destitute. (*sūrah al-Isrā'*, 17:29)

> But as for him who is niggardly, and thinks that he is self-sufficient, and calls the ultimate good a lie – for him shall We make easy the path towards hardship: and what will his wealth avail him when he goes down [to his grave]? (*sūrah al-Layl*, 92:8–11)

> True piety does not consist in turning your faces towards the east or the west – but truly pious is he who believes in God, and the Last Day, and the angels, and revelation, and the prophets; and spends his substance – however much he himself may cherish it – upon his near of kin, and the orphans, and the needy, and the wayfarer, and the beggars, and for the freeing of human beings from bondage; and is constant in prayers, and renders the purifying dues; and [truly pious are] they who keep their promises whenever they promise, and are patient in misfortune and hardship and in time of peril: it is they that have proved themselves true, and it is they, they who are conscious of God. (*sūrah al-Baqarah*, 2:177)

And walk not on the earth with haughty self-conceit: for, verily, thou canst never rend the earth asunder, nor canst thou ever grow as tall as the mountains! (*sūrah al-Isrā'*, 17:37)

For, [true] servants of the Most Gracious are [only] they who walk gently on earth, and who, whenever the foolish address them, reply with [words of] peace; (*sūrah al-Furqān*, 25:63)

Call thou [all mankind] unto thy Sustainer's path with wisdom and goodly exhortation, and argue with them in the most kindly manner:... (*sūrah al-Naḥl*, 16:125)

O my dear son! Be constant in prayer, and enjoin the doing of what is right and forbid the doing of what is wrong, and bear in patience whatever [ill] may befall thee: this, behold, is something to set one's heart upon! (*sūrah Luqmān*, 31:17)

But [since] good and evil cannot be equal, repel thou [evil] with something that is better – and lo! He between whom and thyself was enmity [may then become] as though he had [always] been close [unto thee], a true friend! (*sūrah Fuṣṣilat*, 41:34)

But withal, if one is patient in adversity and forgives – this, behold, is indeed something to set one's heart upon! (*sūrah al-Shūrā*, 42:43)

... those who have attained to faith, and who enjoin upon one another patience in adversity, and enjoin upon one another compassion. (*sūrah al-Balad*, 90:17)

And do not allow your oaths in the name of God to become an obstacle to virtue and God-consciousness and the promotion of peace between men: for God is All-Hearing, All-Knowing. (*sūrah al-Baqarah*, 2:224)[35]

O you who have attained to faith! Do not deprive yourselves of the good things of life which God has made lawful to you, but do not transgress the bounds of what is right: verily, God does not love those who transgress the bounds of what is right:... (*sūrah al-Mā'idah*, 5:87)

Say, "Who is there to forbid the beauty which God has brought forth for His creatures, and the good things from among the means of sustenance?..." (*sūrah al-Aʿrāf*, 7:32)

> O you who have attained to faith! Surrender yourselves wholly unto God, and follow not Satan's footsteps, for, verily, he is your open foe. (*sūrah al-Baqarah*, 2:208)

> O you who have attained to faith! Why do you say one thing and do another? Most loathsome is it in the sight of God that you say what you do not do! (*sūrah al-Ṣaff*, 61:2–3)

ʿAbd Allāh ibn Masʿūd reported that the Messenger of God had said:

> ...beware of lying, for no good can come from lying whether it is done in seriousness or in jest. A [righteous] man would not promise his son something, then fail to keep his promise. Untruthfulness leads to unrighteousness, and unrighteousness leads to hell, whereas truthfulness leads to righteousness, and righteousness leads to paradise. Of the truthful person it is said, "He spoke truly, and he was righteous," and of the untruthful person it is said, "He spoke untruth and was unrighteous." If one of God's servants continues to speak untruth, he will be recorded in God's register as a liar.[36]

Samurah ibn Jundub reported that the Messenger of God had said:

> Two men came to me [during my heavenly ascent] and said, "The man whose jawbone is being split was a liar [during his life on earth]. When he uttered a lie, it was passed on [to others] until it reached the horizons, and thus will he be tormented for his lying till the Day of Resurrection."[37]

In a similar vein, we have the following statement of the Prophet reported by Abū Hurayrah, "There are three signs by which one recognizes the hypocrite: When he speaks, he utters untruth, when he makes a promise, he fails to keep it, and when trust is placed in him, he betrays the trust."[38]

ʿUmar ibn al-Khaṭṭāb, who had sat at the Prophet's feet and whose character had been formed by the Book of God, once avenged a young Copt who had been struck by the son of the Arab commander and prince, ʿAmrū ibn al-ʿĀṣ, then governor of Egypt. Inspired by the example of the Prophet and the Qur'anic perspective on the world, ʿUmar addressed ʿAmrū, his son, and the generations that would follow them in a bold affirmation of the brotherhood and equality of all human beings, saying, "How can you enslave human beings who, when their mothers brought them into the world, were free spirits?"[39] Indeed, how can one human being dare to enslave another when they are brothers in humanity, created by a single Maker, descended from a single soul, and equally worthy of honor and respect?

It should be clear from the foregoing that the Qur'anic perspective views sound human nature as something that entails unity and diversity – balance, integration, and complementarity between the human being as individual and the human being as community. For as we have seen – just as the body has no existence without the members and parts that make it up, nor do its members and parts have any existence or function apart from the body as a whole – so also do the community and the individual need one another in order to survive and to thrive. There is no individual without a family, without a people, without a homeland, without a nation; nor can the individual exist without an awareness of familial, ethnic, national, religious, and human identity and the relationships, associations, and affiliations that they generate in so many concentric and overlapping circles. All of these are fundamental, positive dimensions of the individual's being that help to ensure sound performance, a full existence, growth, and prosperity based on the principles of justice, charity, peace, and the rejection of injustice, corruption, and aggression.

The distinctive feature of the Qur'anic worldview is that, in contrast to a materialistic, racist worldview, it looks upon the differences and distinctions that exist among people as well as the various components of the universe overall as parts of a purposeful divine scheme founded on complementarity and mutual benefit. The ability to perceive differences and distinctions from this positive perspective constitutes the foundation for a harmonious, sound human existence in which we make responsible, loving use of our human and natural resources. There is no room in this perspective for exclusiveness or extremism on either the individual or the communal level; on the contrary, it promotes the pursuit of integration, balance, moderation, and peace in all its dimensions.

Consequently, believers' prayers in the Qur'an do not stop at the concerns of the individual except insofar as such concerns touch upon one's strictly private affairs. Instead, they go beyond the individual to the community, since the best interests of the individual are inseparable from those of the community to which he belongs. We are taught in the Qur'an to pray, saying:

> Thee alone do we worship; and unto Thee alone do we turn for aid. (*sūrah al-Fātiḥah*, 1:5)

> ...O our Sustainer! Accept thou this from us: for, verily, Thou alone art All-Hearing, All-Knowing! "O our Sustainer! Make us surrender ourselves unto Thee, and make out of our offspring" a community that shall surrender itself unto Thee, and show us our ways of worship, and accept our repentance: for, verily, Thou alone art the Acceptor of Repentance, the Dispenser of Grace! (*sūrah al-Baqarah*, 2:127–128)

> And so, they who come after them pray, "O our Sustainer! Forgive us our sins, as well as those of our brethren who preceded us in faith, and let not our hearts entertain any unworthy thoughts or feelings against [any of] those who have attained to faith. O our Sustainer! Verily, Thou art compassionate, a Dispenser of Grace!" (*sūrah al-Ḥashr*, 59:10)

The Qur'anic Worldview is One of World Peace

The final religion came as a source of guidance and as a means of inaugurating the universal, scientific phase of human civilization with its vision of justice, brotherhood, compassion, peace, and creativity. Consequently, the words of the Qur'an were not addressed solely to this or that tribe, people, group, or class. Rather, they were, and continue to be, addressed to humanity at large. Nor is the Qur'an a discourse of the supernatural and the miraculous like the revelations that had been delivered to humanity in earlier periods of its development. Rather, it is the discourse of knowledge, of reading, of reflection, and of contemplation; it is a discourse of reason, argument, and persuasion, of guidance and direction, of brotherhood, justice, and peace. Hence, the Qur'anic worldview and the revelation that embodied it have brought the universal perspective suited to the worldwide scientific phase of humanity's evolution, a phase that best reflects our God-given human nature and the timeless laws of the cosmos, and which goes well beyond the narrow isolationism of the racist, materialistic view of the world that prevailed in the ages of primitive thought and prehistory.

The Qur'anic message of Islam is one that transcends superstitions and the racist, antagonistic inclinations generated by tribalistic, nationalistic mindsets and philosophies and affirms instead the unity of the human race overall. As such, it is capable of guiding humanity by instilling within them those values and principles that are conducive to true security and peace.

Racism, tribalism, and nationalism are exclusive by nature, since their premises and philosophies emphasize aspects of contrast and difference. Differences then become a means of excluding others, claiming superiority to them, and promoting and facilitating conflict and hostility against anyone who is not like 'us.' Hence, the vision of the world founded on differences and negative distinctions fans the flames of conflict and enmity, turning diversity into a basis for hostile confrontations. In so doing, it generates relationships founded on inequality, domination, and opposition among nations, states, and ethnic groups – on account of which recent centuries have witnessed the crimes of colonialism and world wars, which to this day pose a danger to the world's safety through perilous arms races on the part of tyrannical regimes that believe in nothing but power politics and the monopolization of influence and control via deception, manipulation, and fraud.

The Qur'anic worldview is, in reality, the only philosophy and perspective that highlights and affirms the unity of humanity despite the differences that exist among peoples and individuals on virtually all levels:

> ...Behold, We have created you all out of a male and a female, and have made you into nations and tribes, so that you might come to know one another. Verily, the noblest of you in the sight of God is the one who is most deeply conscious of Him... (*sūrah al-Ḥujurāt*, 49:13)

> ...do not covet the bounties which God has bestowed more abundantly on some of you than on others... (*sūrah al-Nisā'*, 4:32)

The Qur'anic worldview is a philosophy that views the various relationships that exist between us and others as complementary rather than competitive, and that calls for them to be governed under all circumstances by a spirit of goodwill, charity, and justice.

The materialistic worldview, by contrast, starts with the individual and his or her ego-driven needs (the 'self that incites to evil'). Consequently, it has given rise to the nationalistic, racist, exclusivist political orientation that has been adopted in modern times especially with the abandonment of religion as a foundation for itself and the rest of the world. This act of abandonment took place in response to the corruption, superstition, and ecclesiastical domination that had made its way into its religious traditions, customs, and culture. It also took place in response to the fact that the religions concerned were tied to bygone historical periods that had lost their relevance to modern life. The materialist view thus turned its back on the spiritual worldview in favor of the materialistic, competitive, conflict-based orientation epitomized in the law of the jungle, where aggressive, group-based solidarity and its interests rule the day. What ensued was an era that witnessed the emergence of various and sundry nationalisms with their resultant self-centered, racist, aggressive, colonialist, brutal power politics. In the name of class struggles across the globe and in every society, the tyrannical, materialist, godless worldview embodied in Marxism has produced a perpetual state of conflict as a result of which both the peoples that have lived under Marxist rule and those around them (particularly the Islamic peoples in Central and East Asia) suffered injustices, oppression, and corruption that led ultimately to the collapse of the Marxist empire from within.

Given the tremendous dangers posed by the materialistic worldview, a "law of the jungle" philosophy if nothing else, and the devastating conflicts, both worldwide and regional, to which it has led – not to mention the existence of weapons of mass destruction and the possibilities they represent – it is vital for the Muslim nation and humanity as a whole to understand, and help others to understand, the Qur'anic worldview as it relates to the building of societies and the fostering of relationships among peoples and nations. Only in this way will we be able to create a culture of justice and peace. However, this understanding must not be superficial or merely theoretical; rather, it needs to be thorough and based on solid facts. It also needs to be educational, applicable to people's emotional and psychological upbringing – both organizational and institutional. In other words, such an understanding needs to be fit to serve as the basis for a peaceful, global human system which affirms that people's beauty, worth and potential lie in their diversity. Given this affirmation, we will be equipped to make responsible use of our human and natural resources and lay the foundations for a society of justice, compassion, and peace.

Sūrah al-Tīn clarifies the relationship that exists between the spiritual aspect of the individual – referred to in *sūrah al-Fajr*, 89:27 as *al-nafs al-muṭma'innah* (the soul 'that has attained to inner peace') – *al-nafs al-ammārah bi al-sū'* (the material, 'animal' aspect or the self 'that incites to evil'), and the role of the human will in purifying the person and enabling that side of human nature, which strives for what is pure, lofty, and righteous to prevail over the side that tends toward decadence, self-gratification, and corruption. This surah begins with a divine oath that stresses the importance of the issue to be dealt with: "Consider the fig, and the olive, and the Mount of Sinai, and this land secure!" (*sūrah al-Tīn*, 95:1–3). This surah deals with the creation of humanity and the relationship between the material and spiritual within the human being: "We have indeed created man in the best of molds." In *sūrah Ṭā Hā*, the following verse speaks of human being's spiritual creation in the world of the spirit in Paradise, where he or she was content and unfettered by needs of any kind:

> And thereupon We said, "O Adam! Verily, this is a foe unto thee and thy wife: so let him not drive the two of you out of this garden and render thee unhappy. Behold, it is provided for thee that thou shalt not hunger here or feel naked, and that thou shalt not thirst here or suffer from the heat of the sun." (*sūrah Ṭā Hā*, 20: 117–119)

However, when Adam disobeyed and gave heed to the powers of evil and corruption embodied in Satan's whisperings and suggestions, thereby incurring God's decree against him, God caused him to descend from the world of spiritual bliss and purity to the world of material, animal existence with its needs, disgraceful acts, and injustices:

> But Satan whispered unto him, saying, "O Adam! Shall I lead thee to the tree of life eternal, and [thus] to a kingdom that will never decay?" And so the two ate [of the fruit] thereof: and thereupon they became conscious of their nakedness and began to cover themselves with pieced-together

> leaves from the garden. And [thus] did Adam disobey his Sustainer, and thus did he fall into grievous error. (*sūrah Ṭā Hā*, 20:120–121)

It was in this way that Adam and his descendents came to combine within themselves both the spiritual and the material: "Verily, We create man in the best of conformation, and thereafter We reduce him to the lowest of low" (*sūrah al-Tīn*, 95:4–5).

Between the world of the spirit, the conscience, and the pursuit of goodness and righteousness on one hand, and the world of matter and self-centered, hedonistic impulses on the other – the role of the human will is to choose between self-purification via the pursuit of justice, reform, and constructive action, and the base, self-serving impulses that manifest themselves in acts of injustice, aggression, and the spread of corruption:

> Thereafter, [however,] his Sustainer elected Him [for his grace], and accepted his repentance, and bestowed His guidance upon him, saying: "Down with you all from this [state of innocence, and be henceforth] enemies unto one another! None the less, there shall most certainly come unto you guidance from Me: and he who follows My guidance will not go astray, and neither will he be unhappy...." (*sūrah Ṭā Hā*, 20:122–123)

In other words, the goodness of humanity, its existence and its civilization on earth depend on the victory of the powers of the spirit through the certainty of faith in the oneness of the Creator, the purposefulness of the creation, and commitment to the ethical constraints inherent in a truly righteous life.

At this point we need to clarify the difference between Islam and the Muslim, and between the call to faith (*al-daʿwah*) and the state (*al-dawlah*). Islam is the final divine message to human beings, which provides us with the foundations of the Qur'anic perspective on the meaning and purposes of human existence and our God-given potentials as stewards and vicegerents on earth. Notwithstanding differences in their circumstances, potentials, and the like, human beings are addressed by the Islamic message in their capacity as God's stewards and representatives on earth. Each one of us takes from the values and teachings of Islam whatever he or she has the capacity and the will to absorb and apply. Then, as our lives and strivings come to an end, be they for good or for evil, we are held accountable for what we have been and done.

As a community, Muslims are people who believe in the fundamentals of Islam and the unchanging truths embodied in its creeds. However, it is up to each individual Muslim – based on his and her own reason, emotions, and will – to determine the morality of his or her behavior and the seriousness with which he or she strives for the good in all things. Hence, as with all groups of people, Muslims will differ from one another in terms of the strength of their faith and commitment and the soundness of their conduct. Therefore, it is a mistake to attribute this or that individual Muslim's behavior to his religion and beliefs. For to the extent that he speaks and acts with integrity and purity, this will be undoubtedly be due to the effect of his religion and its creeds; similarly, to the extent that he departs from the ideals and principles of his religion, this will be due to factors relating to his individual choices and propensities, as well as his upbringing and the understanding he has of his religion's teachings.

Similarly, we must be careful not to confuse the Islamic call to faith, or *daʿwah*, with the Islamic state, or *dawlah*. The *daʿwah* is a discourse addressed to the heart and the conscience for the purpose of assisting, guiding, and teaching; such a discourse must therefore be delivered with gentleness and kindness:

> Whoever chooses to follow the right path, follows it but for his own good; and whoever goes astray, goes but astray to his own hurt; and no bearer of burdens shall be made to bear another's burden.... (*sūrah al-Isrā'*, 17:15)

As for the state, it is a political entity which exists, in one or another of a variety of forms, for the purpose of human social organization. In one way or another, the state has to do with human communities and their sociopolitical systems, their lands, their interests, and their arrangements – both internal or domestic arrangements pertaining to the members of the society in question, and external or international arrangements pertaining to relations with other communities, states, or societies.

Relations between the state and other entities take one of three forms: (1) a state of peace governed by binding principles and laws that order the internal affairs of the political community concerned; (2) a state of covenant and agreement between the political community or state and other communities or states, in which case relations are governed essentially by agreement, commitment to promises made and treaties concluded, and the principle of reciprocity; or (3) a state of conflict, hostility or war, the outcome of which is decided by the balance of power: "...And never let your hatred of people who would bar you from the Inviolable House of Worship lead you into the sin of aggression: but rather help one another in furthering virtue and God-consciousness,..." (*sūrah al-Mā'idah*, 5:2).

The Islamic worldview bases all such relationships on the principle of justice and peace. Within the domestic realm, justice, joint responsibility, and mutual agreement serve as the foundation for all relations, while advisement and mutual consultation are the means by which decisions are made. If relations go awry and injustice is perpetrated, appeal is made to the law, be it secular law or Islamic law. Peaceful means of protest and civil disobedience are the soundest ways of correcting matters and obliging the party or parties who have erred to mend their ways by pulling the rug out from under their feet, so to speak. If, in spite of such measures, the offending party persists in its destructive, aggressive, or disruptive conduct, it must be confronted by the state itself – since it is not acceptable for parties other than the state to take the law into their own hands, thereby entering into violent conflicts that would paralyze the nation and further harm its interests.

As for relations with another political entity, they are to be conducted through negotiation between those in power in order to ensure that the rights of all are respected. War and bloodshed must only be resorted to if it has proved impossible to ensure people's rights by any other means. If war is declared, it must target only those in authority by obliging them to conform their conduct to the truth or by removing them from power. Moreover, if violence is resorted to, it must be kept to the minimum level possible under the circumstances.[40]

It is unfortunate that the West has latched so enthusiastically onto the scientific method, without also accepting the monotheistic Islamic worldview. The West was introduced to the systematic study of the physical sciences through contact with the Islamic world and the Muslim community during the Crusades, the reception of knowledge from Muslim institutes of learning, particularly in Andalusian Spain, as well as the translation of the works of Muslim thinkers into European languages. Western thinkers were guided later to an understanding of the laws and principles on the basis of which human nature and human society operate; as a result of this, they developed the social sciences, albeit from a materialist perspective, which enabled them to construct their societies and institutions on a 'survival of the fittest model,' in which the members of one species (read: 'nationalisms,' 'ethnicities,' and 'cultures') are pitted in solidarity against the members of all others. All of this has served to exacerbate the effects of the West's abandonment of religion due to its having fallen under the sway of formalism and excessive ecclesiastical control – and as a result of which religion in Western societies has almost come to be viewed as a superstition of sorts.

In response to antagonistic misrepresentations of Islam and its Prophet by ecclesiastical authorities anxious to preserve their own narrow interests and corrupt practices, European peoples likewise adopted a hostile stance toward Islam and its founder. Meanwhile, the West inclined increasingly to a materialist, dog-eat-dog mentality and racist bigotries, which served to promote nationalism and its resultant conflicts – attempts at mutual exploitation, aggression, fanaticism, and power politics. The materialist philosophy that gave rise to the foregoing attitudes and practices has served likewise to foment the spread of maladies associated with moral decadence. And to make things still worse, moral laxness and its outcomes have not been viewed as intolerable ethical and social aberrations; rather, they have come to be adopted as the norm: as models of natural, acceptable social conduct and its outcomes. Throughout the West and in liberal societies generally, this development has led to the disintegration of the family and the spread of violence and other social ills, the dangers of which prudent thinkers in the West have been warning against with growing urgency. Yet, even such thinkers, for all their sagacity and insight, have been unable to perceive any way out of the West's predicament, so bound are they to the materialistic worldview they have imbibed for so long.

Regrettably, the era of the rightly guided caliphate was brought to an end and, with it, the possibility of developing viable institutions based on its concepts, perspectives, values, and historic, Qur'an-based leadership models that had found expression in that bygone era. Having imbibed the foundational principles of Islamic culture and the practices that marked earlier Islamic eras, modern Western nations have now succeeded the Muslim nations in carrying the banner of the scientific study of the material and social domains. Hence, as the Muslim community comes to a new awareness of itself and a new recognition of its Qur'anic worldview, it needs to take note of the importance of its institutions and to instill within them the Islamic values of justice, freedom, brotherhood, consultation, constructive action, and peace. For without Islam-based institutions, the powers of base self-interest will gain ascendency once again – dragging the Muslim community anew into the slough of tyranny, corruption, violence, impotence, ignorance, backwardness, and the monopolization of power and wealth.

Given the foregoing, let us state again a proper understanding of the Qur'anic worldview and the structure of its associated social institutions is the starting point for all true reform, peace, and prosperity – not only for the Muslim community, but for humanity at large. However, before undertaking an overview of the principles of the Islamic worldview and methodology, it will be important for us to recall the issue of time and place in understanding the revelation and its written repositories – namely, the Qur'an and the Prophetic Sunnah. Otherwise, we run the risk of confusing constants and variables – or of allowing variables to become constants and constraints, in which case we rob the sacred law of Islam of its comprehensive quality and its ability to provide us with the guidance we need in the circumstances and situations that arise in differing times and places.

Constants and Variables in the Dimensions of Time and Place

Revelation, as the most fundamental source of the religion and its capacity to guide us as human beings, is manifested first and foremost in the Holy Qur'an, which is the word of God revealed to His noble Messenger. The Qur'an is a final, universal divine message which bears the character of an unchanging reality. What this means is that it is a message that conveys aims, values, and concepts that remain constant over time, and from one place to another. These aims, values, and concepts are what we are referring to as 'constants'; an example of such constants are fatherhood and sonhood – and the bonds, rights, and duties that are associated with them.

Because the conditions of human life – as well as human knowledge, potentials, needs, and challenges – are in a state of continual flux and evolution, the applications of Islamic values and concepts must also change and evolve in keeping with the realities of people's lives, which change from one era to another, and vary from one place to another. As for the role of the Messenger of God as the final Prophet, it lay in being the model who provides definitive evidence that the Qur'an is not a book of fanciful, idealistic conceptions or dreams, but rather a message of guidance to be applied to the rough-and-tumble of everyday life and its practices. Hence, in addition to his responsibility to deliver the message he had been given and to call others to the truth with kindness and goodly exhortation, his mission was to apply the values embodied in the message he had been given. In this way, he demonstrated that the guidance he had brought was directly relevant to the reality of people's lives, and that it was to be assimilated by each individual, community, and generation in accordance with their particular capacities and understandings.

Sound application of Islamic values and concepts within the context of particular times and places requires wisdom, knowledge, and discernment. Hence, the ways in which the Prophet – as the builder of a society and head of state – applied the values and concepts of the Qur'an to his particular circumstances offer a model for others as they seek to reapply these values and concepts to their own changing, evolving times and places. The application of the principles of mutual consultation (*al-shūrā*) to and in the era of transportation on the backs of donkeys and mules, for example, is bound to differ from their application to the age of electronics, air travel, and communication via e-mail and the Internet. Herein, lies the significance of the lessons to be derived from the life and example of the Prophet, because Islam has a relevance that will be ongoing until the Day of Judgment:

> Alif. Lām. Rā. A divine writ [is this], with messages that have been made clear in and by themselves, and have been distinctly spelled out as well – [bestowed upon you] out of the grace of One who is Wise, All-Aware. (*sūrah Hūd*, 11:1)

> Indeed, God bestowed a favor upon the believers when he raised up in their midst an apostle from among themselves, to convey His messages unto them, and to cause them to grow in purity, and to impart unto them the divine writ as well as wisdom – whereas before that they were indeed, most obviously, lost in error. (*sūrah Āl ʿImrān*, 3:164)

Hence, we must realize the nature of the sources of the religion, including both its constants and its variables. For if the Qur'an is the word of God and His final message to humankind, it follows, therefore, that it is the source of valid guidance in the proper use of nature and the laws of the cosmos in all times and places.

As for the role of the Prophetic Sunnah as a second source of the Islamic message, it consists in manifesting the wisdom required in the application of the values, principles, and concepts of this message and the fulfillment of its aims in time and place, and in making clear to people that the message of the Qur'an is not some fanciful, idealistic set of notions, but rather a message of concrete guidance for humankind. Herein, we find the reason for the divine preservation of the Qur'an. At the same time, we begin to understand why the Messenger of God commanded those who had recorded any part of the Sunnah in writing to strike it out, since the purpose of the Sunnah had already been fulfilled by pointing to the practical nature of the Qur'anic teachings and by manifesting the wisdom required for their application in place and time. Through the Prophetic Sunnah, we see that the application of the Qur'an is by nature something which changes and evolves with changes in people's circumstances, knowledge, potentials, and challenges.

Given the foregoing, we can better understand why it is that, although the Messenger of God took care to ensure that his commands, statements, and actions in relation to the management of the affairs of state and society during his lifetime were not recorded and preserved in written form – nevertheless, in his capacity as head of state, he insisted on the necessity of others obeying his commands. He insisted that his commands be carried out, since what he was commanding, though not in the Qur'an, was an application thereof to the circumstances in which he and his community found themselves. If, however, the Prophet's instructions had been placed on a par with the Qur'an itself, this would have led to a confusion between the enduring, conceptual nature of the Qur'an, which has relevance to all times and places – and his own conduct and applications, which had relevance to his own location and time in particular. In other words, the Messenger of God sought to make clear that we are not to apply the teachings of the Qur'an in a rigid, literal fashion that conforms precisely to the ways in which it was applied during his lifetime; rather, we are to cultivate an awareness of the temporal and geographic variables that apply to our own situations, and to take these variables into consideration when applying the Qur'an to our own time and location.

In light of the foregoing, we can understand why the rightly guided Caliph ʿUmar ibn al-Khaṭṭāb instructed some of the Companions who had gone to other cities and regions not to speak with those around them about certain sayings and actions of the Prophet – since, unlike the inhabitants of Madinah, people elsewhere would not be familiar with the circumstances that had provided the occasions for many of these actions and sayings and, as a result, there was a risk of them not understanding them properly. Thus, the necessary foundations for the reconstruction of our educational curricula are: an understanding of the nature of the Qur'an and the Prophetic Sunnah, a knowledge of human nature and the laws of the cosmos, and an awareness of particular people's circumstances with their potentials and challenges.

Given this analysis of the issue of time and place as it relates to the nature of Qur'anic concepts and the Prophetic Sunnah, we now proceed to a discussion of the principles of the Qur'anic worldview and a sound Islamic mindset.

A Realistic Idealism

Is the worldview conveyed through the Qur'an and the life of the Prophet a purely idealistic vision on the order of a philosopher's utopia? Is it merely an intellectual luxury that has no place in the details of people's daily lives? Or is it a realistic message capable of guiding people to what is best for them by enabling the forces of goodness in the human soul to overcome inclinations toward hedonism, evil, injustice, and self-interest?

On first consideration, it is difficult to imagine a positive answer to this question, particularly in light of many aspects of the reality being experienced at present by the Muslim community, which has witnessed deterioration in its social fabric, its political and economic systems, its conduct, and its relationships with others. In short, the reality being lived at present by the Muslim nation appears to be at complete odds with the guidance embodied in the message and vision conveyed in the Holy Qur'an.

In order to answer the question being posed, we need first to bring to mind a number of premises. The first of these premises is that there is nothing in the Qur'anic worldview which does not answer to the longings of the human heart. The second premise is that the era of the Prophet was the concrete model that conformed fully to the Qur'anic vision, as a result of which people could see its realism and the possibility of achieving it in place and time thanks to the forces of goodness, righteousness, spiritual aspiration, and creativity inherent in the human soul. And the third of these premises is that there are inevitable disparities among individuals and societies in terms of their capacity to apply the values and concepts of goodness, reform, and cultural progress to their individual conduct and communal structures. Therefore, societies or communities in which the forces for good, justice, and constructive action are relatively weak need not despair of their ability to reform themselves and to set themselves on a positive, constructive course.

The starting point for such a process is for the Muslim community to recognize that it has regressed, and that these developments have taken place for identifiable reasons which can be treated and dealt with. Such a recognition need not discourage the Muslim community in its efforts to reform itself and to regain its footing. On the contrary, it is through such honesty and realism that the forces of goodness and reform can be released anew. Since utopian idealism is one thing, and realistic idealism is another, the Muslim community must learn to turn a deaf ear to ignorant or biased claims to the effect that what Islam calls us to be and do is unrealistic.

At the same time, idealism can only be of value if it has ways of dealing with the human self – its complex makeup, its aspirations, and its inclinations on the concrete, temporal level. Otherwise, humanity is bound to retreat into the darkness of its base, materialistic impulses – into racism, conflict, mutual attempts at exploitation, cruelty, bloodshed, and aggression in the name of 'realism.' Meanwhile, the acceptance of all manner of human decadence and depravity will be justified based on the claim that every reform and every attempt to rein in the forces of evil and injustice is romantic idealism and nothing more. Hence, a realistic idealism offers humanity its only hope of deliverance from further regression into the darkness of crass materialism and its woes.

The second part of the question raised earlier concerning the idealistic nature of the Qur'anic worldview is: does this mean that in order to live up to this Qur'anic idealism, the Muslim is required to apply all Islamic values, concepts, and principles in all areas of his or her life and behavior, in his or her every waking moment, every day of his of her life? In other words, in order for a person to be Muslim, must he or she be infallible and invulnerable to sin and temptation? As we have had occasion to note, the language of threat and intimidation into which Islamic discourse has slipped has reinforced this perception and belief – which has in turn caused the Qur'anic worldview, seen within the context of the current cultural realities of the Muslim community, to appear well-nigh impossible of attainment.

Moreover, given what we know of human nature, which is a veritable battleground for opposing forces – material and spiritual, good and evil, altruistic and egocentric – it goes without saying that error and sin are part and parcel of the human experience, and that there is no basis for the belief that anyone (except God's messengers and prophets) could be infallible in any area of life whatsoever.

"Every human being is a sinner, and the best of sinners are those who turn to God in repentance."[41] What this means is that deep within every one of us is a spiritual nature and a moral force that impels us to seek wisdom, goodness, charity, and righteousness. However, our physical needs and our baser proclivities tempt us to be drawn into the commission of injustice, indecent acts, and aggression. When this happens, sound-minded people's consciences and spiritual affinities pursue them and condemn them for the evil or indecent acts they have committed. The Qur'anic worldview confirms the reality of this inward struggle, teaching us how to cope with it and enable the forces of good within us to overcome our baser drives.

The psychological struggle that takes place within the individual between the forces of goodness and the forces of evil is a universal reality. Similarly, both the longing for goodness and righteousness and the possibility of error and sin are ingrained within our very nature. However, seen from the perspective of the Qur'anic worldview, this is no cause for frustration or despair. On the contrary, this struggle can be best dealt with by supporting the forces of goodness in the soul and not despairing of one's ability to correct whatever has gone awry. For God, who has imbued us with moral failings as well as with virtue and consciousness of Him (*sūrah al-Shams*, 91:8), is the Most Compassionate, the Most Merciful, and the Most Generous, who receives those who, having fallen due to weakness, ignorance, or necessity, repent and turn away from error and sin. Indeed, the door is open to every remorseful, repentant individual, and once one has repented and returned to God, the slate is wiped clean as though one had never gone astray.

It is thus important to draw a distinction between the Qur'anic worldview, which is a source of guidance, support, and reinforcement for the forces of goodness, reform, and forward movement in the human soul, and the human assimilation of this perspective with its associated values, concepts, and principles. The reason for this distinction, as we have seen, is the conflict that takes place within the individual due to the rival forces and currents at work within each of us, which make it possible for us to err and lose our way. This conflict can be dealt with, however, through an awareness of the situations and circumstances that cause individuals, nations, and civilizations to stumble and fall, followed by conscious efforts at reform.

In order for reform and lasting change to take place, we will need to take some critical, penetrating looks at our cultures, our discourses, and the ways in which we raise our children and train our workforce. Once we have done this, our vision will be corrected, our thinking will become sound, and our emotions and wills will be purified. Then, as we seek to meet our needs and achieve our interests as individuals and as a community, the predominant orientation among us will be the desire for what is good and right. Error and wrongdoing will be an exception that is decried by the community, and that the individual finds so repugnant that even if he succumbs to temptation, he will readily repent and turn away from it.

Muslim thinkers, reformers, and educators are called upon to identify the ills that afflict present-day Islamic culture, its ways of thinking, its approaches to childrearing and professional training, its educational curricula, and its institutions. Similarly, each subgroup within the wider Muslim community is called upon to recognize the sources of the malfunction or imbalance within it and methods of correcting it. However, when this takes place, the community will be able to regain its health and its role as a cultural pioneer with a clear vision and a sense of hope and optimism. The Qur'anic worldview will again serve as the basis for the community's way of life, and consequently, it will not be diverted from its mission by slips and errors. Rather, the societal forces that reject and confront such errors will possess a renewed capacity for revitalization and empowerment in the life of the community, and for the development and improvement of its institutions. As we read in the Holy Qur'an:

> And yet, I am not trying to absolve myself: for, verily, man's inner self does incite [him] to evil, and saved are only they upon whom my Sustainer bestows His grace. Behold, my Sustainer is Much-Forgiving, a Dispenser of grace! (*sūrah Yūsuf*, 12:53)

> and who, when they have committed a shameful deed or have [otherwise] sinned against themselves, remember God and pray that their sins be forgiven – for who but God could forgive sins? – and do not knowingly persist in doing whatever [wrong] they may have done. These it is who shall have as their reward forgiveness from their Sustainer, and gardens through which running waters flow, therein to abide: and how excellent a reward for those who labor! (*sūrah Āl ʿImrān*, 3:135–136)

As we build our lives and pass through its various stages, be they fruitful or barren, trouble-free or trying, we need to bear in mind that Islam provides a sound perspective on human existence. As such, it is a lifeboat that will bring us safely to shore, a compass that will ensure our secure arrival at our journey's end. Understand that:

- Islam is not a form of racism that caters to human pride or base, aggressive instincts.
- Islam is not a naive, enslaving, humiliating, monastic idealism.
- Islam is not a nihilistic materialism founded on the survival of the fittest.
- Rather, Islam is a down-to-earth yet spiritual idealism that is both balanced and healthy.

This vision of Islam provides a basis for meeting human needs in an atmosphere of safety, justice, and peace of mind. As such, the Islamic vision celebrates and enhances life, leading us to the means of achieving a happy, sound human existence.

Sex, for example, is the springhead of life and the means of its continuation. Therefore, Islam celebrates and affirms sex, while at the same time stressing the importance of bearing the responsibilities it carries with it and protecting the rights of all parties involved. Science and knowledge are one of the sources of civilization, progress, and creativity; hence, Islam encourages the sciences and the pursuit of knowledge in all areas of life, while insisting that knowledge and scientific discoveries be used in ways that are beneficial rather than harmful. Similarly, earning a living and seeking to acquire the means of earthly enjoyment are welcomed by Islam; however, the means employed toward these ends must be legitimate and honorable, devoid of any sort of injustice, deceit, or overindulgence. Life has no meaning without freedom and the protection of human rights, dignity, and honor. Therefore, Islam insists on the protection and defense of human freedoms and rights, while forbidding hostility and aggression and encouraging pardon and forgiveness wherever possible.

No sound, healthy behavior poses hardship for someone who has a clear, sound vision of things and has been given a healthy upbringing. If there is any difficulty or hardship, it results in most cases from the distorted worldview that has shaped one's social milieu and led to decline and corruption in its culture and educational system. In such situations, both individuals and nations have the responsibility to confront whatever crises are being faced by the society rather than attempting to evade the issues on the pretext of a sham idealism or so-called realism. The issue, once again, is one of vision; it is a matter of mindset, culture, and educational approach in all their dimensions as well as the numerous factors that go to make them up and activate them. Hence, it makes no sense for the Islamic religion or its associated worldview to be scapegoated for human inadequacy and negligence. Nor can we disregard the true reasons for the crisis – be they subjective or objective, internal or external – or allow the forces of darkness and ignorance to exercise their sway over society and hinder efforts to bring about change.

CHAPTER II

THE PRINCIPLES EMBODIED IN THE QUR'ANIC WORLDVIEW

IT is essential that we understand the universal values and principles embodied in the Qur'anic worldview and their implications for human life and culture. For these values and principles represent the fundamental, essential building blocks by means of which the Qur'anic worldview is manifested on the practical level. They mold the mindset of the Muslim community and the individual Muslim, who then translate them into concrete realities. In this way, they guide the cultural progress of the society – supplying its members with the strength, will, and energy they need in order to be effective in their performance, to achieve their aims, and to grow and develop in such a way that they keep pace with evolving circumstances, potentials, and challenges and humanity's developing knowledge and understanding of the world.

Monotheism

Monotheism, that is, the affirmation that there is only one Absolute, is the most fundamental principle of the Islamic worldview, since it provides the most intuitively convincing, universal response to human beings' spiritual need and their longing to understand both their origin and their destiny. In addition, it represents the 'ceiling' of human logic in understanding the various dimensions of life and existence:

> ...there is nothing like unto Him, and He alone is All-Hearing, All-Seeing. (*sūrah al-Shūrā*, 42:11)

> Nay – who is it that creates [all life] in the first instance, and then brings it forth anew? And who is it that provides you with sustenance out of heaven and earth? Could there be any divine power besides God?... (*sūrah al-Naml*, 27:64)

> Did you, then, think that We created you in mere idle play, and that you would not have to return to Us? [Know,] then, [that] God is sublimely exalted, the Ultimate Sovereign, the Ultimate Truth: there is no deity save Him, the Sustainer, in bountiful almightiness enthroned! Hence, he who invokes, side by side with God, any other deity [- a deity] for whose existence he has no evidence – shall but find his reckoning with his Sustainer: [and,] verily, such deniers of the truth will never attain to a happy state! (*sūrah al-Mu'minūn*, 23:115–117)

> had there been in heaven or on earth any deities other than God, both [those realms] would surely have fallen into ruin! But limitless in His glory is God, enthroned in His awesome almightiness [far] above anything that men may devise by way of definition! (*sūrah al-Anbiyā'*, 21:22)

The unity, almighty power, uniqueness, and perfection of the Creator and the exquisite complementarity to be observed in the creation not only explain, but even necessitate the unity, diversity, harmony, and completeness of the created universe. They explain the marvelous orderliness to be observed in the universe and necessitate both its purposefulness and the moral principles on the basis of which it operates:

> Verily, in the creation of the heavens and the earth, and in the succession of night and day, there are indeed messages for all who are endowed with insight, [and] who remember God when they stand, and when they sit, and when they lie down to sleep, and [thus] reflect on the creation of the heavens and the earth: O our Sustainer! Thou hast not created [aught of] this without meaning and purpose. Limitless art Thou in Thy glory! Keep us safe, then, from suffering through fire! (*sūrah Āl ʿImrān*, 3:190–91)

> ...for it is He who creates everything and determines its nature in accordance with [His own] design. (*sūrah al-Furqān*, 25:2)

The aforementioned verses from the divine revelation point to the visible evidence of the oneness of the Creator. This evidence consists in the exquisiteness of the creation, its integrative unity, its orderly, systematic structure, the causality we observe in events and phenomena, and the moral purposefulness of the cosmos.

In addition, the instructions given to us in the Qur'an reflect the essential nature of the human conscience with its purposeful, ethical, spiritual inclinations. These inborn propensities of the human conscience manifest themselves in the values of goodness, truth, justice, brotherhood, solidarity, mercy, and peace – without which life and existence and its marvelous order, from the subatomic particle to the galaxy, would have no meaning. Without these values, the concept of a meaningful life and existence give way to a belief in chaos and nihilism, which is inconsistent with the orderliness of the world we live in, human intuition, and common sense. As God Almighty declares:

> ...I have not created the invisible beings and men to any end other than that they may [know and] worship Me. [But withal,] no sustenance do I ever demand of them, nor do I demand that they feed Me: for, verily, God Himself is the Provider of all sustenance, the Lord of all might, the Eternal! (*sūrah al-Dhāriyāt*, 51:56–58)

> Now whoever surrenders his whole being unto God, and is a doer of good withal, has indeed taken hold of a support most unfailing: for with God rests the final outcome of all events. (*sūrah Luqmān*, 31:22)

Just as the integrated nature of the universe and the masterly perfection of its order necessitate the unity and almighty power of its Maker, so also do they explain and necessitate the causal unity and harmony of the creation itself:

> Verily, in the creation of the heavens and of the earth, and the succession of night and day: and in the ships that speed through the sea with what is useful to man: and in the waters which God sends down from the sky, giving life thereby to the earth after it had been lifeless, and causing all manner of living creatures to multiply thereon: and in the change of the winds, and the clouds that run their appointed courses between sky and earth: [in all this] there are messages indeed for people who use their reason. (*sūrah al-Baqarah*, 2:164)

Systematic scientific study reveals the magnificence, vastness, harmony, and precision of the universe as manifested in the depths of the sea, on the face of the earth, and in the far-flung galaxies in outer space. As such, it helps us to be conscious of the logic of material existence or physical reality – as well as what lies beyond physical reality, that is, the metaphysical realm. Such a consciousness lends existence another dimension and points to another logic that differs from the logic of either the material realm or of the human mind:

> He [alone] knows that which is beyond the reach of a created being's perception, and to none does He disclose aught of the mysteries of His Own unfathomable knowledge, (*sūrah al-Jinn*, 72:26)

> ...you have been granted very little of [real] knowledge. (*sūrah al-Isrā'*, 17:85)

The realization of such things imbues the believer and the scientist with a new humility, such that they take seriously their lives in this world and their God-given task of being upright, trustworthy stewards of the creation. With this attitude, the Muslim believer achieves self-realization and attains happiness and self-esteem in this world – while, at the same time, being reassured of his destiny when, in the life to come, the whole picture becomes visible to him:

> they know but the outer surface of this world's life, whereas of the ultimate things they are utterly unaware. (*sūrah al-Rūm*, 30:7)

> But nay, you prefer the life of this world, although the life to come is better and more enduring. (*sūrah al-Aᶜlā*, 87:16–17)

> And every human being will come forward with [his erstwhile] inner urges and [his] conscious mind, [and will be told:] "Indeed, unmindful hast thou been of this [Day of Judgment]; but now We have lifted from thee thy veil, and sharp is thy sight today!" (*sūrah Qāf*, 50:21–22)

Divinely-given Stewardship

The principle of divinely granted stewardship is reflected in God's statement to the angels upon His creation of human beings:

"...Behold, I am about to establish upon earth one who shall inherit it..." (*sūrah al-Baqarah*, 2:30). This principle is derived not merely from a Qur'anic command, but rather from human nature itself, that is, from the characteristics and abilities that God has planted within us. On both the individual and the communal levels, human beings possess awareness, understanding, and the spirit which is the seat of our God-given human nature. These capacities are related in turn to the human conscience and the desire to seek knowledge and understanding –both of which qualify human beings to be stewards or vicegerents of God who are distinguished from other creatures by their ability to make decisions, act, and make use of their environment in order to meet their needs and give concrete expression to their values, visions, and aspirations. After all, matter has no value unless it embodies sound values and principles – nor do principles, values, and visions have any merit unless they find concrete expression in matter.

Hence, the principle of stewardship, which implies the ability to act in the world, bestows an honored position on human beings, who are called upon to distinguish between the various creatures that surround them. This position entails both the right to exercise freedom in the making of life decisions, and duties, responsibilities, and accountability for our actions and the ways in which we have put our abilities and energies to use on earth:

> Verily, We have shown him the way: [and it rests with him to prove himself] either grateful or ungrateful. (*sūrah al-Insān*, 76:3)

> Have We not given him two eyes, and a tongue, and a pair of lips, and shown him the two highways [of good and evil]? But he would not try to ascend the steep uphill road... (*sūrah al-Balad*, 90:8–11)

Thus. it can be seen that stewardship, with all that it entails by way of the privilege of acting and the responsibility of decision making, lies at the heart of human life and its purpose:

> God has promised those of you who have attained to faith and do righteous deeds that, of a certainty, He will cause them to accede to power on earth, even as He caused [some of] those who lived before them to accede to it; and that, of a certainty, He will firmly establish for them the religion which He has been pleased to bestow on them;... (*sūrah al-Nūr*, 24:55)

Justice and Moderation

If monotheism – with all that it implies by way of moral purposefulness, order, harmony, and complementary in the universe – is the foundation and point of departure for the Qur'anic worldview, and if stewardship means the ability to make conscious decisions and to make responsible use of the material world and all that this implies by way of accountability, then justice is the central aim of all human action and interaction and on all levels: the material and spiritual, the economic, the social, and the political. Without justice, and with it moderation, all dimensions of human existence and stewardship are emptied of meaning and purpose, since it is justice that serves as the measuring rod for sound human conduct. For this reason, justice is the first thing human beings are commanded to pursue. God Himself has committed Himself to justice, and when human beings go astray by allowing their wills to become enslaved to anything other than God and His perfect law, they wrong only themselves:

> Behold, God enjoins justice, and the doing of good, and generosity towards [one's] fellow-men; and He forbids all that is shameful and all that runs counter to reason, as well as envy; [and] He exhorts you [repeatedly] so that you might bear [all this] in mind. (*sūrah al-Naḥl*, 16:90)

> These are God's messages: We convey them unto thee, setting forth the truth, since God wills no wrong to His creation. (*sūrah Āl ʿImrān*, 3:108)

Because justice lies at the heart of the meaning and goodness of life, God directs human beings to find fulfillment through the pursuit of justice and moderation in all things – even if one must do so to one's own harm; nor must one deny justice to anyone, even one's enemy. God says:

> Say: "I believe in whatever revelation God has bestowed from on high; and I am bidden to bring about equity in your mutual views. God is our Sustainer as well as your Sustainer. To us shall be accounted our deeds, and to you, your deeds...." (*sūrah al-Shūrā*, 42:15)

> O you who have attained to faith! Be ever steadfast in upholding equity, bearing witness to the truth for the sake of God, even though it be against

> your own selves or your parents and kinsfolk. Whether the person concerned be rich or poor, God's claim takes precedence over [the claims of] either of them. Do not, then, follow your own desires, lest you swerve from justice: for if you distort [the truth], or refuse to testify, behold, God is indeed aware of all that you do! (*sūrah al-Nisā'*, 4:135)

The Qur'an helps us to see the all-inclusiveness of justice – in all aspects of life, for both the individual and the community – including social justice and what it necessitates by way of compassion, cooperation, and solidarity when it praises those "and in whose possessions there is a due share, acknowledged [by them], for such as ask [for help] and such as are deprived [of what is good in life];" (*sūrah al-Maᶜārij*, 70:24–25). Similarly, God commands us in the Qur'an, saying, "...Eat of their fruit when it comes to fruition, and give [unto the poor] their due on harvest day. And do not waste [God's bounties]: verily, He does not love the wasteful!" (*sūrah al-Anᶜām*, 6:141).

If justice is the core of a wholesome life, then moderation is the evidence of justice. The reason for this is that an absence of moderation is a kind of excess that leads to corruption in people's lives, as well as in the environment. As such, immoderation is a transgression against justice. Hence, there is no justice without moderation. If justice prevails, moderation is bound to prevail as well, and if moderation reigns, justice, compassion, and solidarity are sure to reign along with it. God commends those "and who, whenever they spend on others, are neither wasteful nor niggardly but [remember that] there is always a just mean between those [two extremes];" (*sūrah al-Furqān*, 25:67). God also says:

> And give his due to the near of kin, as well as to the needy and the wayfarer, but do not squander [thy substance] senselessly. Behold, the squanderers are, indeed, of the ilk of the satans – inasmuch as Satan has indeed proved most ungrateful to his Sustainer. (*sūrah al-Isrā'*, 17:26–27)

> And thus have We willed for you to be a community of the middle way, so that [with your lives] you might bear witness to the truth before all mankind, and that the Apostle might bear witness to it before you.... (*sūrah al-Baqarah*, 2:143)

In a similar vein, Wā'ilah ibn al-Asqaᶜ once asked the Prophet, "O Messenger of God, what is bigotry?" To which the Prophet replied, "Bigotry is to aid your own people in the commission of injustice."[1]

Kaᶜb ibn ᶜUjrah said, "The Messenger of God said, 'After me there will be rulers who are untruthful and unjust. Those who believe their lies and aid them in their wrongdoing have nothing to do with me, nor I to do with them, and they will not drink with me from the blessed pool in Paradise.'"[2] Similarly, Jābir ibn ᶜAbd Allāh related that the Messenger of God had said, "Beware of committing injustice, for injustice will lead one into darkness on the Day of Resurrection. And beware of miserliness, for miserliness destroyed those who came before you by leading them to shed one another's blood and disregard the sacredness of what is sacred."[3]

In a *ḥadīth qudsī* quoted earlier, God declared on the lips of the Prophet, "O My servants, I have forbidden injustice to myself and have likewise rendered it forbidden among you. Therefore, commit no injustice against one another."[4]

And in *Saḥīḥ al-Bukhārī*, we read that the Messenger of God said, "Injustice will lead one into darkness on the Day of Resurrection."[5]

Freedom

As thinking, creative, social beings, humans are set apart from other creatures by their position as God's stewards on earth. Moreover, they have been qualified for the task of stewardship by their ability to engage in conscious action and make use of the earth's resources in order to meet their varied and increasing needs and reap the benefits and pleasures offered by the world around them. As God Almighty declares, "Now, indeed, We have conferred dignity on the children of Adam, and borne them over land and sea, and provided for them sustenance out of the good things of life, and favoured them far above most of Our creation:" (*sūrah al-Isrā'*, 17:70).

Human beings are distinguished from other creatures by the fact that they possess a spirit and a conscience:

> And lo! Thy Sustainer said unto the angels: "Behold, I am about to create mortal man out of sounding clay, out of dark slime transmuted; and when

> I have formed him fully and breathed into him of My spirit, fall down before him in prostration!" Thereupon the angels prostrated themselves, all of them together, save Iblīs: he refused to be among those who prostrated themselves. (*sūrah al-Ḥijr*, 15:28–31)

They are also distinguished by their desire to seek knowledge as well as the potentials and abilities such knowledge makes possible for them:

> And He imparted unto Adam the names of all things; then He brought them within the ken of the angels and said, "Declare unto Me the names of these [things], if what you say is true." They replied, "Limitless art Thou in Thy glory! No knowledge have we save that which Thou hast imparted unto us. Verily, Thou alone art All-Knowing, Truly Wise." Said He: "O Adam, convey unto them the names of these [things]." And as soon as [Adam] had conveyed unto them their names, [God] said, "Did I not say unto you, 'Verily, I alone know the hidden reality of the heavens and the earth, and know all that you bring into the open and all that you would conceal'?" (*sūrah al-Baqarah*, 2:31–33)

Through the distinguished position human beings have been granted in the order of creation and the stewardship-relevant capacities that set them apart from other creatures, we see the divine honor that has been bestowed upon them. This honor entails a responsibility, which in turn requires that human beings enjoy the freedom to make meaningful choices and give concrete expression to their convictions and desires within the limits of their abilities, potentials, and circumstances on both the individual and communal levels: "God does not burden any human being with more than he is well able to bear..." (*sūrah al-Baqarah*, 2:286), and "...God does not burden any human being with more than He has given him..." (*sūrah al-Ṭalāq*, 65:7). However, freedom is not a justification for chaos or for toying with the rights and interests of other individuals, the community, or coming generations.

Hence, no one is permitted to infringe upon this human right of stewardship in its individual and communal dimensions or to place restrictions on people's striving for the good. On the contrary, the divine honor bestowed on human beings requires that their right to make free choices be protected – for only in this way will they be able to carry out their stewardship-related responsibilities, and only in this way can they be held ultimately accountable for their actions in this world.

At this point, it is important to make clear that there are two kinds of freedom. The first kind is a subjective personal freedom, a freedom of the conscience having to do with an individual's convictions, doctrinal beliefs, and worldview. One person may offer advice to someone else or invite him to consider other ways of looking at things. However, no one has the right to impose his own perspectives and convictions on anyone else or to interfere in this aspect of another person's life.

As for the second type of freedom, it is the freedom to act within the social sphere. Given the way it impacts the various members of society, this freedom has corresponding limits which are determined through mutual consultation. Any member of the society has the right to fulfill his or her personal aims without hindrance –provided that this freedom does not turn into a kind of social chaos that allows for unsound conduct that would bring harm to the interests of other individuals or the interests of the society at large, whether directly or indirectly, in the short term or the long term:

> And when they are told, "Do not spread corruption on earth," they answer, "we are but improving things!" (*sūrah al-Baqarah*, 2:11)

However, if restrictions are imposed on individual freedoms in response to the dictates of special interests, the society will fall into the clutches of corruption or the tyranny of those possessed of power and wealth:

> And say: "The truth [has now come] from your Sustainer: Let, then, him who wills, believe in it, and let him who wills, reject it." (*sūrah al-Kahf*, 18:29)

> And so, [O Prophet,] exhort them; thy task is only to exhort: thou canst not compel them [to believe]. (*sūrah al-Ghāshiyah*, 88:21–22)

> There shall be no coercion in matters of faith. Distinct has now become the right way from [the way of] error:... (*sūrah al-Baqarah*, 2:256)

The story of the prophet Abraham, illustrates the intuitive nature of monotheistic belief, as well as its purposefulness and its morality. By virtue of the nature of human existence, communal life and the community provide the framework for individual movement and freedom. The Qur'an provides us with the following account:

> And indeed, long before [the time of Moses] We vouchsafed unto Abraham his consciousness of what is right; and We were aware of [what moved] him when he said unto his father and his people, "What are these images to which you are so intensely devoted?" They answered: "We found our forefathers worshipping them." Said he: "Indeed, you and your forefathers have obviously gone astray!" They asked: "Hast thou come unto us [with this claim] in all earnest – or art thou one of those jesters?" He answered: "Nay, but your [true] Sustainer is the Sustainer of the heavens and the earth – He who has brought them into being: and I am one of those who bear witness to this [truth]!" And [he added to himself,] "By God, I shall most certainly bring about the downfall of your idols as soon as you have turned your backs and gone away!" And then he broke those [idols] to pieces, [all] save the biggest of them, so that they might [be able to] turn to it. [When they saw what had happened,] they said: "Who has done this to our gods? Verily, one of the worst wrongdoers is he!" Said some [of them]: "We heard a youth speak of these [gods with scorn]: he is called Abraham." [The others] said: "Then bring him before the people's eyes, so that they might bear witness [against him]!" [And when he came,] they asked: "Hast thou done this to our gods, O Abraham?" He answered: "Nay, it was this one, the biggest of them, that did it: but ask them [yourselves] – provided they can speak!" And so they turned upon one another, saying, "Behold, it is you who are doing wrong." But then they relapsed into their former way of thinking [and said]: "Thou knowest very well that these [idols] cannot speak!" Said [Abraham]: "Do you then worship, instead of God, something that cannot benefit you in any way, nor harm you? Fie upon you and upon all that you worship instead of God! Will you not, then, use your reason?" (*sūrah al-Anbiyā'*, 21:51–67).

During the critical phase of rebuilding the Muslim community, it needs to be remembered that humans have no real existence merely as individuals, since people are by nature social beings. In other words, they exist essentially as a community. As the Qur'an reminds us, God has distributed blessings among people in differing proportions "...to the end that they might avail themselves of one another's help..." (*sūrah al-Zukhruf*, 43:32). The individual is only able to achieve self-realization in the context of a larger group to which he or she belongs. Hence, by virtue of the nature of human existence, communal life and the community provide the framework for individual movement and freedom. Ultimately, then, it is the community that determines what boundaries and controls are needed in order to release the individual's potentials and creative energies; in so doing, it should strive for the proper balance between individual rights and freedoms, and the right of the community to ensure its well-being and survival. The achievement of such a balance requires a harmonious, consultative approach whose aim is to serve people's best interests and protect them from harm and tyranny. The Qur'an assures us that God's enduring reward shall be given to those "and who respond to [the call of] their Sustainer and are constant in prayer; and whose rule [in all matters of common concern] is consultation among themselves;..." (*sūrah al-Shūrā*, 42:38). The purpose of consultation is to provide guidance for the ordering and management of society as a whole without infringing on individual rights and freedoms:

> O mankind! Be conscious of your Sustainer, who has created you out of one living entity, and out of it created its mate, and out of the two spread abroad a multitude of men and women. And remain conscious of God, in whose name you demand [your rights] from one another, and of these ties of kinship. Verily, God is ever watchful over you! (*sūrah al-Nisā'*, 4:1)

Responsibility

By virtue of their inborn spiritual perception and affirmation of God's oneness, their intuitive awareness of the purposeful nature of the universe, and their acknowledgement of moral values, people are led both rationally and intuitively to the conviction that within the limits of their abilities and circumstances, they enjoy the freedom to make meaningful choices for which they must bear responsibility:

> On the Day of Resurrection people will be told, "Today, then, no human

being shall be wronged in the least, nor shall you be requited for aught but what you were doing [on earth]." (*sūrah Yā Sīn*, 36:54)

...We do not burden any human being with more than he is well able to bear: for with Us is a record that speaks the truth [about what men do and can do]; and none shall be wronged. (*sūrah al-Mu'minūn*, 23:62)

And be conscious of the day on which you shall be brought back unto God, whereupon every human being shall be repaid in full for what he has earned, and none shall be wronged. (*sūrah al-Baqarah*, 2:281)

On the Day when God will raise them all from the dead and will make them truly understand all that they did [in life]: God will have taken [all of] it into account, even though they [themselves] may have forgotten it – for God is witness unto everything. (*sūrah al-Mujādalah*, 58:6)

But We shall set up just balance-scales on Resurrection Day, and no human being shall be wronged in the least: for though there be [in him but] the weight of a mustard-seed [of good or evil], We shall bring it forth; and none can take count as We do! (*sūrah al-Anbiyā'*, 21:47)

Whoever shall come [before God] with a good deed will gain ten times the like thereof; but whoever shall come with an evil deed will be requited with no more than the like thereof; and none shall be wronged. (*sūrah al-Anʿām*, 6:160)

Purposefulness

It will be clear from the foregoing that purposefulness is a principle that inheres necessarily in the concept of an ordered universe, the notion of the oneness of the Creator, and the oneness and complementarity to be observed in the cosmos. Given the natural human tendency to believe in the oneness of the Divine and to sense one's responsibility for the sound use of the earth's resources, as well as the perceptive capacities and knowledge with which we have been endowed, we are led to the conviction that the cosmos must necessarily be purposeful in nature. A thoughtful examination of the world around us makes it very difficult to imagine its having come into existence by mere chance; nay, it is difficult to imagine it having come into existence without the agency of an all-powerful, perfectly wise Being who represents another dimension, and another logic that far surpasses human reason, knowledge, and imagination. As we are reminded by the words of the Qur'an:

> But nay! I call to witness all that you can see, as well as all that you cannot see! (*sūrah al-Ḥāqqah*, 69:38–39)

> And [know that] We have not created the heavens and the earth and all that is between them in mere idle play: [for,] had We willed to indulge in a pastime, We would indeed have produced it from within Ourselves – if such had been Our will at all! (*sūrah al-Anbiyā'*, 21:16–17)

> Did you, then, think that We created you in mere idle play, and that you would not have to return to Us? (*sūrah al-Mu'minūn*, 23:115)

How cruel and trivial life would be if it were nothing but a quest for physical survival and passing enjoyments, at the end of which one became a lifeless corpse to be buried and forgotten. If this were the case, life would be no more than an illusion, and neither reason, nor conscience, nor choice, nor responsibility, nor creative capacities would have any ultimate significance. It is both absurd and counterintuitive to think of human beings – with their capacity for reason, moral accountability, and creativity and their desire to strive for righteousness, virtue, and a world where right is might, that is, where power arises from the commitment to truth – as equal to animals that lack all such capacities and who live by the law of the jungle, where might is right.

The Qur'anic worldview sees human life as a serious, meaningful venture of fundamental goodness. Moreover, it sees the fruit of all we accomplish in this life by way of reform, creativity, and service, as extending into the spiritual realm of eternity. As such, human life goes beyond the death of the body to an everlasting spiritual existence in which human beings reap the fruits of all they have done. God Almighty declares:

> Indeed, unto God belongs all that is in the heavens and all that is on earth: and so He will reward those who do evil in accordance with what they did, and will reward those who do good with ultimate good. (*sūrah al-Najm*. 53:31)

> For those who persevere in doing good there is the ultimate good in store, and more [than that]. No darkness and no ignominy will overshadow their faces [on Resurrection Day]: it is they who are destined for paradise, therein to abide. (*sūrah Yūnus*, 10:26)

Self-realization through pursuit of the good on both the material and spiritual levels is an innate aspiration that forms a part of our God-given nature. Conversely, the pursuit of evil, harm, and corruption is blameworthy and despicable and, therefore, something that our God-given nature abhors.

Morality

Human beings' innate awareness of the existence of a single, Almighty, unique Creator who made the universe with infinite precision and wisdom, as well as the lofty spiritual values implanted within the human spirit and conscience, enable them to realize that the universe has to have a divine origin as well as a purpose. Conversely, they realize that the cosmos with its vast and varied dimensions could not have been created in mere caprice; on the contrary, it must have been brought into existence for lofty moral purposes. This inborn spiritual perception is the foundation for the religious and moral sense, as well as the spiritual longings, aspirations, and questions that begin to manifest themselves from the time when a young child first becomes aware of his surroundings. Such longings, moreover, are reflected in and satisfied by the Qur'anic worldview. By bringing such aspirations into the center of our awareness, the Qur'anic worldview guides us in such a way that it becomes our focus and a source of inspiration which elevates our minds and hearts and blesses us with inner peace and happiness in the course of our endeavors. Based on the Qur'anic worldview one becomes better able to make conscious, well-informed, responsible decisions concerning the direction one will take in life and what destiny one seeks: will it be the path of reform, constructive action, and the well-being they engender – or will it be selfishness, greed, corruption, and the misery they bring? As the Qur'an reminds us concerning those who chose the latter path and met with ruin, "...It was not God who wronged them, but it was they who had wronged themselves" (*sūrah al-ʿAnkabūt*, 29:40).

> Verily, in the creation of the heavens and the earth, and in the succession of night and day, there are indeed messages for all who are endowed with insight [and] who remember God when they stand, and when they sit, and when they lie down to sleep, and [thus] reflect on the creation of the heavens and the earth: "O our Sustainer! Thou hast not created [aught of] this without meaning and purpose. Limitless art Thou in Thy glory! Keep us safe, then, from suffering through fire!" (*sūrah Āl ʿImrān*, 3:190–191)

The Islamic worldview intensifies our awareness of our responsibility and moral accountability, which are inseparable parts of our God-given human nature and among the features that qualify us to fulfill the role of God's stewards on earth. In so doing, it guides the course of our lives in such a way that we are able to achieve genuine self-realization and spiritual fulfillment as individuals who are integral parts of a wider human community and who strive responsibly and with dignity for the legitimate pleasures this life has to offer and honor in the life to come.

Just as human beings, both individually and communally, are honored through their position as God's stewards and through the freedom they have been granted, so also do they bear a responsibility to act in the universe in such a way that they become agents of reform and progress. At the same time, they achieve self-realization by obtaining what they need through constructive, ethical means and by seeking justice, charity, and peace. In so doing, they allow their conduct to be governed by their God-enlightened consciences, thereby demonstrating that right is might. God Almighty declares:

> Verily, We did offer the trust [of reason and volition] to the heavens, and the earth, and mountains: but they refused to bear it because they were afraid of it. Yet man took it up – for, verily, he has always been prone to be most wicked, most foolish. (*sūrah al-Aḥzāb*, 33:72)

> And most certainly have We destined for hell many of the invisible beings and men who have hearts with which they fail to grasp the truth, and eyes with which they fail to see, and ears with which they fail to hear. They are like cattle – nay, they are even less conscious of the right way: it is they, they who are the [truly] heedless! (*sūrah al-Aʿrāf*, 7:179)

Mutual Consultation

According to the Qur'anic worldview, human beings were created to be God's stewards on earth and to carry out the task of populating and developing the earth:

> ...Behold, I am about to establish upon earth one who shall inherit it.... (*sūrah al-Baqarah*, 2:30)

> ...He brought you into being out of the earth, and made you thrive thereon. (*sūrah Hūd*, 11:61)

Hence, by virtue of their growing knowledge, human beings have been given the ability to make use of the earth's resources and to build cultures and civilizations. They have also been granted freedom, the ability to choose, a capacity for spiritual and moral perception that leads them to live purposefully and to seek goodness and rectitude, and an awareness of their accountability before their Maker:

> Consider the human self, and how it is formed in accordance with what it is meant to be, and how it is imbued with moral failings as well as with consciousness of God! To a happy state shall indeed attain he who causes this [self] to grow in purity, and truly lost is he who buries it [in darkness]. (*sūrah al-Shams*, 91:7–10)

> [For,] would We treat those who have attained to faith and do righteous deeds in the same manner as [We shall treat] those who spread corruption on earth? Would We treat the God-conscious in the same manner as the wicked? (*sūrah Ṣād*, 38:28)

It must be remembered, of course, that although the task and mission of stewardship is an individual responsibility, it is first and foremost a communal and social responsibility that is passed down from one generation to the next. This fact lends significant dimensions to freedom and human responsibility. To begin with, responsibility is purposeful – its aim being reform and constructive development, not corruption and destruction. Similarly, freedom is not some chaotic, unbounded nihilism. For although freedom allows for personal, subjective convictions and individual choices, it must not be allowed to harm other individuals or violate their rights; nor should it be permitted to violate the right of the community to pursue reform and development. In short, the existence of the individual and his or her performance as a steward of God are inseparable from the existence of the community and its social functions.

Consequently, although the individual enjoys the undisputed right to his or her personal convictions as well as the right to act on such convictions, these individual rights must not be allowed to infringe on the community's right to security, prosperity, and order. This being the case, the community possesses the right to legislate controls for the regulation of individual conduct in order to protect communal interests, rights, and aspirations for development and reform, be they short-term or long-term:

> ...In this way God makes clear His messages unto you, so that you might find guidance, and that there might grow out of you a community [of people] who invite unto all that is good, and enjoin the doing of what is right and forbid the doing of what is wrong: and it is they, they who shall attain to a happy state! (*sūrah Āl ᶜImrān*, 3:103–104)

Herein lies the importance of mutual consultation (*al-shūrā*), which is not subject to the whims or interests of individuals with influence and power but which, rather, is open to the participation of the wider community. Mutual consultation exists for the purpose of protecting the legitimate rights of all to act on the basis of their convictions without hindrance or restriction, thereby fulfilling the purpose of human existence and serving their shared goals of development, reform, and security. Mutual consultation is thus essential for the well-being of the individual, the community, and the entire human race.

A careful examination of the Qur'an pertaining to the concept of mutual consultation and its vital link to stewardship-related, ethical, and developmental aims reveals the true meaning of rightly-guided freedom exercised in a spirit of fairness, dignity and tolerance. God states:

> And [remember that] whatever you are given [now] is but for the [passing] enjoyment of life in this world – whereas that which is with God is far

> better and more enduring. [It shall be given] to all who attain to faith and in their Sustainer place their trust; and who shun the more heinous sins and abominations; and who, whenever they are moved to anger, readily forgive; and who respond to [the call of] their Sustainer and are constant in prayer; and whose rule [in all matters of common concern] is consultation among themselves; and who spend on others out of what We provide for them as sustenance; and who, whenever tyranny afflicts them, defend themselves. But [remember that an attempt at] requiting evil may, too, become an evil: hence, whoever pardons [his foe] and makes peace, his reward rests with God – for, verily, He does not love evildoers. Yet indeed, as for any who defend themselves after having been wronged – no blame whatever attaches to them: blame attaches but to those who oppress [other] people and behave outrageously on earth, offending against all right: for them there is grievous suffering in store! But withal, if one is patient in adversity and forgives – this, behold, is indeed something to set one's heart upon! (*sūrah al-Shūrā*, 42:36–43)

Mutual consultation is thus a principle whose purpose is to ensure healthy, effective human functioning, a tool for stimulating sound human thought and arriving at mature, communally thought-out convictions, and a means of promoting open communication, moderation, and tolerance. As such, mutual consultation serves as a shield that protects the community from the evils of tyranny, authoritarianism, injustice, and corruption. Supported by the Qur'anic worldview – with its mutual consultation and the maturity it fosters, as well as its ethical concepts and values – and an awareness of its interests and its legitimate right to determine its own life choices, the Muslim community can claim its rightful mandate over those in power and become the force that directs and oversees them, not vice versa. Otherwise, those in power oversee and control the citizenry. Treating the populace as though they were incompetent and ignorant, leaders may exploit them for their own interests and the interests of their devotees – monopolizing power and wealth, and annihilating all potential for competence, creativity, growth, and constructive competition in their governments and societies. Therefore, freedom and mutual consultation (or the lack thereof) play a significant role in the rise and fall of civilizations.

Freedom and Consultation as Necessary Conditions for the Survival of Human Civilization

It goes without saying that authoritarianism, injustice, and corruption cannot coexist with freedom and the practice of mutual consultation. If such evils taint any social structure, it cannot be said to be truly free and based on mutual consultation. The society of a free people whose thinking and vision have been brought to maturity through the exercise of genuine freedom and open discussion could never be tainted with tyranny, injustice, and corruption. For such evils only germinate and grow in the darkness of ignorance and deception; after all, if people are free and in open communication on all levels, it will be impossible to mislead all of them all of the time. Thus, it is that justice is the fruit of freedom and mutual consultation, and that freedom and mutual consultation cannot exist without justice.

As Muslim communities pass through the phase of revival and the recovery of their cultural vitality, they need to appreciate the interdependence that exists between freedom and mutual consultation on one hand, and the rise and fall of civilizations on the other. Similarly, they need to understand how Muslim thinkers, leaders, and reformers can deal with the reality that now faces them, and work toward rehabilitating the Muslim community in such a way that it can reclaim its place, its mission, and its unique position in the progress of human civilization.

When the cancer of tyranny and corruption has begun to eat away at a civilization's way of thinking and its social system, its economic and social structure are undermined and there arises a parasitic class of sorts that monopolizes power, resources, and wealth to the point where the entire civilization collapses, thereby paving the way for the rise of a new, pioneering civilization which is founded on the remains of the civilization that preceded it. The nascent civilization is able to see cultural and developmental possibilities and opportunities that its predecessor civilization – calcified as it was by the tyranny and corruption under whose yoke it had been laboring – was no longer able to perceive and make the most of. Thus, it is that young, newly emerging nations can move toward new, broader scientific and cultural horizons which moribund civilizations are no longer able to reach or even perceive.

This type of cultural calcification and inertia sets in when oppression and tyranny get the better of a nation's life system. When this takes place, the pharaonic political institution subjugates the nation's thinkers and intellectuals, turning them into little more than a domesticated intelligentsia whose function is to justify the status quo by misleading the people with a distorted worldview, thereby molding the public's will in conformity with that of the ruling regime. Be it secular or religious, the intellectual class thus becomes a tool in the hands of the new pharaohs who hold the reins of power:

> Art thou not aware of how thy Sustainer has dealt with [the tribe of] ʿĀd, [the people of] Iram the many-pillared, the like of whom has never been reared in all the land? – and with [the tribe of] Thamūd, who hollowed out rocks in the valley? and with Pharaoh of the [many] tent-poles? [It was they] who transgressed all bounds of equity all over their lands, and brought about great corruption therein: and therefore thy Sustainer let loose upon them a scourge of suffering: for, verily, thy Sustainer is ever on the watch! (*sūrah al-Fajr*, 89:6–14)

> Have they, then, never journeyed about the earth and beheld what happened in the end to those [willful] sinners who lived before their time? God destroyed them utterly: and the like thereof awaits all who deny the truth. (*sūrah Muḥammad*, 47:10)

Human civilization today suffers from the supremacy of materialism and racism (the self that incites to evil), sham democracy and its claims, so-called freedoms that are nothing more than a facade for nihilistic anarchy, the media's misleading talking heads, and phony research centers controlled by the influential, moneyed class. These phenomena – together with the monopolies, injustices, ignorance, impoverishment, extravagance, excess, and destruction to which they lead – are bound to drive humanity to perdition unless the dawn of a spiritual, Islamic civilization breaks anew.

The fine minds that have emigrated from other lands, and which for over a century have lent advanced nations a temporary youthful vigor at the expense of the poor and oppressed nations from which they came, will be unable to rescue modern materialistic civilization from the distortions and falsehoods manifested in its thought and worldview.

Advanced materialistic societies have despoiled other nations' material and human resources in an attempt to escape the effects of their own waywardness, the inflexibility of their political, social, and economic systems, their corrupt, classist, racist practices, and the deteriorating morality of their peoples and social systems. The price of this sophisticated despoliation is paid, of course, by weaker, less advanced nations through the loss of their most enlightened minds, their material and human resources, and their dignity.

The growing seriousness of the maladies that afflict modern-day materialistic societies can be seen in the fact that they have begun to begrudge the influx of individuals from poorer nations, even those with gifted minds. The reason for this is that multinational corporations (the new pharaohs), which are controlled by the feudal lords (monopolies) of the age of scientific and technological wealth (intellectual, technological, industrial, banking, and financial property) and their capitalistic banking mechanisms, have – thanks to the phenomenon of globalization – extended their influence over the entire globe. In this way, they have been able to transform weaker, less advantaged peoples into slaves or 'serfs' in the service of their 'feudal' lords, while preventing them from acquiring knowledge of advanced technologies and gaining access to their secrets. This process is evidenced by rampant injustice, exploitation, and political, social, and economic conflicts throughout the world. Indeed, the present situation is far worse than the control once exercised by the feudal lords of the Middle Ages, who seized exclusive control over medieval agricultural economies.

The effect of capitalistic and technological monopolization is not restricted to underdeveloped and oppressed nations; rather, it has expanded through the outsourcing of many laborious, poorly paid industrial jobs to poverty-stricken nations, as a result of which poverty and the woes of unemployment have spread to the peoples living in advanced nations as well. In this way, the gap between the masses of common people and the feudalistic (monopolistic) minority represented by the techno-capitalist intelligentsia grows ever wider. What this means is that social rigidity and economic, social, and political struggles will continue to worsen and spread throughout the entire world. In fact, this is already taking place, and is threatening human civilization with total destruction. Consequently, reformers need to take the task of rescuing and reviving the Muslim community through a revival of its Qur'anic worldview – and, with it, human civilization as a whole – with utmost seriousness. For otherwise, a dark future awaits us all.

The question now is: will it be possible for the Muslim community's thinkers and reformers to appreciate the dynamism of cultural progress and, in so doing, to extricate their community from the abyss of fossilization and backwardness and help its members to regain an authentic, vital Islamic vision of goodness and forward movement?

It is unfortunate that, for historical reasons related to the nature of its environment and its lack of cultural sophistication, the Muslim community has failed in the past, and particularly in the foundational period immediately subsequent to the death of the Prophet, to realize the importance of institutions. Due to the critical circumstances in which it found itself, the Muslim community did not cope well with the hostility and aggression with which it was met on the part of surrounding empires, nor was there sufficient time for it to discover the critical role that institutions might have played in meeting such challenges. Today, however, if we truly wish to be of service to ourselves and the human community as a whole, we have no excuse for failing to build the best institutions we possibly can. As we are reminded by the Qur'an:

> ...If God had not enabled people to defend themselves against one another, corruption would surely overwhelm the earth: but God is limitless in His bounty unto all the worlds. (*sūrah al-Baqarah*, 2:251)

> God has promised those of you who have attained to faith and do righteous deeds that, of a certainty, He will cause them to accede to power on earth, even as He caused [some of] those who lived before them to accede to it; and that, of a certainty, He will firmly establish for them the religion which He has been pleased to bestow on them; and that, of a certainty, He will cause their erstwhile state of fear to be replaced by a sense of security – [seeing that] they worship Me [alone], not ascribing divine powers to aught beside Me.... (*sūrah al-Nūr*, 24:55)

Areas of certain Islamic countries have suddenly been able to enjoy exorbitant wealth – a wealth that was poured out suddenly upon them out of a divine storehouse of natural resources. Such states – whose rulers are by and large traitorous, ineffectual, corrupt, tyrannical, and greedy – occupy strategic locations as a result of which they have been drawn all too willingly into alliances with foreign powers, which in return for the assistance they provide, have imposed unspoken obligations on the recipient states. Hence, the wealth now possessed by such Islamic states actually threatens to thwart initiatives to move the Muslim community along the path of renewal. This being the case, we may find ourselves on the verge of a new phase of calcification that effectively does away with the harbingers of renewal that began to emerge in the late eighteenth century through Ottoman attempts at reform in Turkey, Muhammad Ali's reform efforts in Egypt, and bursts of reform activity on the Arabian Peninsula, in India, in North Africa, and elsewhere in the Islamic world. Such gratuitous wealth, both monetary and natural, not to mention the dubious conflicts of interests resulting from foreign loans and commissions, has become a source of narcissism, rigidity, tyranny, corruption, and waste. Such phenomena may in turn serve to perpetuate the monopolization of power and wealth and do away with constructive, healthy competition, development, initiative, and creativity. Instead, we find officially sanctioned ignorance, passivity, subservience, poverty, and backwardness in a worn-out, lifeless social structure in which abilities and potentials are stunted, vision, thought, and education are off course, and institutions are corrupt and ineffectual.

If Muslim thinkers, reformers, and educators fail to take note of this possibility, there is a real danger that the first signs of an awakening on the part of the Muslim community will be nipped in the bud before they have the chance to flourish and bear fruit. Will the proper action be taken to rescue the Muslim community from further waywardness and prepare it truly for the opportunity to lay claim to its rightful cultural and spiritual heritage and, in so doing, right the course of human civilization as a whole? Will we recover our Qur'anic worldview with all the blessing it holds for us? Will we do away with the distortions in our thought, our discourse, and our educational methods? Will we build up our institutions in such a way as to protect the values, principles, and beliefs inherent in our Islamic worldview? Will we respect ourselves, protect our freedoms, and establish institutions that promote learning, knowledge, justice, mutual consultation, solidarity, security, and peace as the mainstays of our life as a believing community and our modern-day civilization?

Given the earnest efforts of thinkers, reformers, and educators – together with mothers' and fathers' heartfelt concern and sacrifices on behalf of their children – the Muslim community possesses everything it needs in order to accomplish these goals despite the obstacles before us. For regardless of the influence and authority wielded by modern-day 'pharaohs,' the doubletalk of today's 'soothsayers,' and the clamor raised by their devotees, it is parents who will ultimately win their children over if they have the proper determination and vision. In order for us to be fully qualified for our role as stewards, we must strive for a comprehensive understanding of the cosmos and the laws that govern it. Having done this, we can reap the benefits of our God-given stewardship through commitment to reform, development, and the responsible use of our human and material resources in order to meet human needs, satisfy people's legitimate desires, and develop their creative potentials to the fullest.

Law-governed Scientific Comprehensiveness

God has honored human beings with the capacity to make decisions, take action, and thereby serve as responsible, accountable stewards. In addition, He has given us the ability to perceive His oneness and the unity, complementarity, purposefulness, and moral foundation of the universe, an instinctual desire to pursue knowledge, and the inclination to develop the created world and put its resources to use in such a way that we achieve self-realization, meet our basic needs, and give expression to our individual longings and creative urges. In all these processes, we are called upon to use the God-given gift of reason, which enables us to discern the most prudent use of the earth's blessings. These truths were understood and articulated centuries ago by the illustrious judge and jurisprudent Ibn Khaldūn (d. 808/1406), who contributed to the establishment of systematic, causal, scientific investigation and a systematic, causal approach to the social sciences.

In order for revelation and the various messages in which it has been embodied to be recognized truly as revelation and enter the realm of human knowledge, each messenger's claims and message must first be weighed in the balance of human reason and measured by the criteria of sound logic.[6]

It is important to remember in this connection that causality and responsible stewardship are inseparable. Without causality, life would be reduced to chaos, and there would be no basis for responsible action or accountability. The task of being God's stewards involves the will; as such, it entails responsibility and the capacity for action based on the principles of monotheism, purposefulness, and morality. Denial of causality, by contrast, is a denial of the facts of life, since it is a disavowal of the human capacity for conscious action and the conscious use of the world around us, and this is in turn a disavowal of the Origin of the Cosmos. All of us have observed the fact that without water, there will be no crops or livestock, that without fertilization and pollination, there will be no flowers or fruits, and that without air and the ability to breathe, neither man nor beast would survive. Similarly, without thought and action, there will be no productivity or development.

God-given stewardship of the earth would thus be impossible without a recognition of causality in human life. As God Almighty has said:

> ...Set thy face steadfastly towards the [one ever-true] faith, turning away from all that is false, in accordance with the natural disposition which God has instilled into man: [for,] not to allow any change to corrupt what God has thus created – this is the [purpose of the one] ever-true faith; but most people know it not. (*sūrah al-Rūm*, 30:30)

> ...Our Sustainer is He who gives unto everything [that exists] its true nature and form, and thereupon guides it [towards its fulfillment]. (*sūrah Ṭā Hā*, 20:50)

In the proper relationship between revelation (that which is written, or *al-masṭūr*), the laws of human nature and the cosmos (that which is observed, or *al-manẓūr*), and reason (the balance or scale, or *al-mīzān*) – the laws of human nature and the cosmos are the subject of which the revelation speaks, while the fundamentals of reason and logic are the means by which we understand what guidance the revelation offers us. Hence, through the proper use of reason, we are able to relate in the most fitting and constructive way to ourselves, to our fellow human beings, and to the divinely established patterns and laws of the universe.

If the Muslim way of thinking had not gone off track under the influence of Greek thought (with its myths, make believe and gnostic, mystical flights of fancy), Muslims would have been the first to discover the social sciences. After all, it is they who – by virtue of the timeless, enlightened, scientific worldview given expression in the Qur'an – are the most eminently qualified to master the various social, physical, and technical sciences. By virtue of their early adoption of a law-governed perspective and a comprehensive, scientific approach, they could have achieved far more than other nations have in virtually all the aforementioned fields.

In order to right the course of Islamic thought and culture today, it will be necessary for Muslim thinkers and reformers to reclaim the God-given ability to view themselves and the cosmos from a comprehensive, scientific point of view. Then, based on the solid foundation provided by the Qur'anic worldview, they can set about reforming the Muslim community's approach to culture, education, and child rearing, which together form the basis for the community's way of thinking, its academic institutions, and the training received by its academic workforce and leaders. The aim of such reform is to unify the Islamic perspective on the various fields of human knowledge and areas of life through attentiveness to sound human instincts and the divinely established patterns and laws of the universe. Such reform would facilitate the creation of curricula for a variety of academic specializations to be offered alongside Qur'an-based doctrinal instruction reflecting the Islamic worldview. Through such a dual approach, progress can be made toward instilling an inclusive perspective in the minds and hearts of Muslim youth such that they develop wholesome, constructive aims and aspirations that contribute to the overall well-being of their societies.

A genuinely Islamic worldview is down-to-earth, comprehensive, law-governed, positive, and disciplined. Unfortunately, however, the predominant worldview among Muslims, which purports falsely to be

'Islamic,' is theoretical, atomistic, passive, and selective – its purpose being to justify or conceal a quasi-sacerdotal distortion of knowledge and the facts and the inability to master a comprehensive, objective scientific approach to research and analysis. This type of pseudo-Islamic perspective is reflected in a tendency to appeal to poorly authenticated texts from the Islamic tradition in a polemical, selective manner. Those who engage in this practice want to take refuge in the alleged sanctity of a glorified past in order to conceal their own impotence and rigidity and silence the general populace. The result, however, is a fractured, compartmentalized Muslim community in which the majority of our scholars live in one realm, the majority of our intellectuals in another realm, and the majority of our lay people – many of whom are either isolated, alienated, ignorant, deluded, or the victims of rank superstition – in still another.[7]

Human decisions are influenced not only by knowledge and rational comprehension, but by the heart and the emotions as well. The latter represent psychological and spiritual dimensions that are affected to a large extent by the nature of an individual's education and upbringing. Moreover, it is this non-intellectual dimension of the human being which releases one's energies and potentials, and which serves as the determining force behind the choices an individual makes. In the final analysis, then, it is this dimension that tends to tip the scales in favor of a person's going in one direction rather than another. God says:

> But if the truth were in accord with their own likes and dislikes, the heavens and the earth would surely have fallen into ruin, and all that lives in them [would long ago have perished]!... (*sūrah al-Mu'minūn*, 23:71)

> [And We said:] "O David! Behold, We have made thee a [prophet and thus, Our] vicegerent on earth: judge, then, between men with justice, and do not follow vain desire, lest it lead thee astray from the path of God:..." (*sūrah Ṣād*, 38:26)

Hence, interest in the intellectual aspect of knowledge alone – without concern for its psychological, spiritual, and emotional dimensions – is not sufficient to prepare human beings to bear their God-given responsibilities and to make effective use of their abilities and potentials, since action requires not only knowledge, but rather a response on the part of one's will and emotions to the knowledge one possesses.

Reform movements have largely failed to revive the Muslim masses and deal effectively with the flaws in the Muslim community's societal structures since their educational methods, both in the school and in the home, do not develop the character of Muslim citizens in such a way that they develop mature, effective hearts and consciences. God says:

> Have they, then, never journeyed about the earth, letting their hearts gain wisdom, and causing their ears to hear? Yet, verily, it is not their eyes that have become blind—but blind have become the hearts that are in their breasts! (*sūrah al-Ḥajj*, 22:46)

> Will they not, then, ponder over this Qur'ān? – or are there locks upon their hearts? (*sūrah Muḥammad*, 47:24)

> Nay, but their hearts are corroded by all [the evil] they were wont to do! (*sūrah al-Muṭaffifūn*, 83:14)

> ...God seals the hearts of those who deny the truth;... (*sūrah al-Aʿrāf*, 7:101)

> ...God sets a seal on every arrogant, self-exalting heart. (*sūrah Ghāfir*, 40:35)

> ...Give, then, this glad tiding to [those of] My servants who listen [closely] to all that is said, and follow the best of it: [for] it is they whom God has graced with His guidance, and it is they who are [truly] endowed with insight! (*sūrah al-Zumar*, 39:17–18)

Hence, in order for the Muslim community to recover the Qur'anic worldview and rebuild a system of rightly guided Islamic thought, we need to recognize that sound human instincts, the laws of the universe, and the realities of time and place on one hand, and revelation on the other hand, are the sources of Islamic knowledge. The former provide us with observable facts, while the latter gives true expression to these facts – placing them in the center of our awareness and, in this way, guiding our instincts and the choices we make with our God-given freedom. As for the senses, they serve as tools of reason, which is the measure of human thought. Based on logic and the fundamentals of reason and common sense, we make observations and comparisons that enable us to form judgments about the world. Then, in interaction with our conscience, emotions, and store of life experiences, these judgments move the will,[8] which is the motive force behind all human action. The will serves as the basis for one's choices and decisions, either in pursuit of righteousness, justice, and reform on earth – or in satisfaction of selfish whims and aggressive, self-serving ends, all of which lead one astray from the path of truth and goodness.

Consequently, in order for reform efforts to bear fruit, it is not enough for us to be concerned with the education our children receive in school. Rather, we need to be equally concerned about the education they receive in the home, since a child's upbringing in this area constitutes the basis for his or her psychological formation. As such, it is one of the most critical factors in a human being's life, since it leaves an indelible mark on one's heart, conscience, and emotions by forming the fundamental character traits that he will carry with him throughout life. It is these character traits which direct a person's choices and the way in which he uses his store of objective knowledge in response to concrete situations. As a result, we find that someone might know the right thing to do but not do it; conversely, someone might know that something is wrong, yet do it anyway. Similarly, we may find someone to be apathetic and unmoved at a time when, judging from the seriousness of the situation in which he finds himself and the dire consequences of inaction, one would expect him to fly into a rage. On the other hand, the same person might lose his temper or take radical measures in response to a situation in which, in view of the outcomes of acting in such a way, it would have been wiser to remain calm and self-controlled.

Hence, it is vital that, both as individuals and as a society, Muslims repair what is broken in their way of thinking and the thinking of future generations. This will involve reforming their educational methods, their approach to childrearing, and the way in which they address children's emotional needs. Only in this way will they be able to build the community's future on a foundation of love, understanding, healthy habit formation, inward conviction, courage, self-confidence, and a sense of self-confidence and dignity. As a precondition, as well as an outcome, of these processes, the Qur'anic worldview – the foundation for sound spiritual growth and knowledge – must be revived and nurtured. As a result, the Muslim community will be able to recover the purity of doctrinal belief, the positive, constructive outlook, and the moral probity that characterized the early Muslim generations, thereby laying the foundation for an enlightened Muslim mentality and conscientious, rightly guided action.

Globalism

Globalism is the feature of the phase in which all the various stages of human development come together to form interpenetrating circles of nearness and belonging – from the individual to the family, from relatives to neighbors, from the clan or tribe to the nation, to race – ending at last with the grand, original circle, which is our common humanity. Globalism is the twin sibling of a maturing human civilization with maturing scientific abilities. Such maturation has already eliminated many barriers of time and place, since the globalism of which it is the manifestation calls for nothing less than a discourse addressed to other human beings as brothers and sisters. After all, the world of globalism has no place for racism and provincialism, just as the scientific, law-governed understanding of the world, which has contributed to the emergence of universalism, has no place for superstition or delusion.

All the religions that preceded Islam were messages to particular peoples, who lived a primitive existence in relative isolation from each other. Moreover, the means through which these religions reached the peoples for whom they were intended was largely that of miracles. We can see the effects of the emphasis on the miraculous and the supernatural in the ancient religions that have survived to the present day – such as Hinduism (which originated among the people of India), Confucianism (which began among the people of China), Shintoism (an indigenous Japanese religion), and Judaism (which originated among the people of Israel). In fact, the Prophet Jesus also came performing miracles as a messenger to 'the lost sheep' of the people of Israel.

As for Islam, it came as a message for people all over the world, to all the descendents of Adam. As a consequence, its discourse is addressed to all of humanity, and the means by which it reaches its hearers is a law-governed, scientific understanding of the universe and human beings' place in it. Its message came in the form of a book ("Read!" said the angel Gabriel to the Prophet Muhammad), and its aims were justice and peace. For without justice there can be neither peace nor globalism. Conversely, where there is justice, knowledge, universality, and peace, there is no place for deceit, bigotry, wrongdoing, or aggression; rather, one is called to act justly toward others in an atmosphere of brotherhood, freedom, fairness, understanding, security, and peace. It should be understood, therefore, that globalism and peace are to be distinguished from globalization, hegemony, and exploitation.

It is commonly believed that globalization is something new. However, anyone who has studied economics and the history of the modern-day economy will realize that globalization is nothing but an old, stale concoction being served up in new bottles and under a new name. In reality, it is simply a manifestation of a colonialist, exploitative urge that moves the dominant economic powers of the world – who, armed with the wealth already at their disposal, storm through more barriers of place and time in order to commit even more wrongdoing, injustice, and exploitation at the expense of the weak and dispossessed.

This form of globalization thrives on an economic exploitation that serves the interests of the existing global powers. On the pretext of economic freedom (while at the same time erecting trade barriers for their own economic protection), the neocolonialist powers set out to vanquish the weak powers and despoil their material and human resources by means of military, economic, and cultural hegemony. As a consequence, the subjugated peoples and countries become nothing more than a source of raw materials, cheap labor, and available markets for the dominant neocolonialist states.

If the industries of the neocolonialist powers are stronger than their competitors in other countries, they preach the gospel of 'economic freedom' and support opening up the markets of those countries that fall under their influence, since in this way they can exploit these countries by flooding them with their own products. If, on the other hand, the dominant states find that their industries are in a position of relative weakness in relation to their foreign competitors – in order to maintain their dominant position in the world economy, they pull out the 'economic protection' card and seek to close their markets, as well as those of their satellite countries, in the face of their competitors. A brief glance at the conflicts that have taken place among the colonialist European empires, and particularly the history of the British Empire, will make clear the types of exploitative policies such empires have adopted in pursuit of their unsavory ambitions.

Globalization today is the same call for economic freedom for the superpowers, the ulterior motive for which appears to be to open the way for such powers to engage in even greater exploitation, control, and monopolization. This time, however, these processes are occurring on a much wider and more sinister scale than they have in the past. Making maximum use of space-age electronic gadgets, satellite communications, and the massive military and economic means at their disposal – not to mention the growing worldwide infatuation with such modern-day technological capacities – the superpowers have invaded weaker nations' cultural and economic spheres with exponential success and ease, all the while benefiting from everything that might lure less advantaged peoples into a stupor of relaxation, obsessive consumption, and social and moral chaos.

Even when today's economic superpowers call for 'economic freedom,' they insist on 'protecting' their own weak industries and products. Hence, while they call for so-called 'freedom,' they negotiate with one another behind the scenes to guarantee themselves the needed 'protections' and exceptions. At the same time, however, they refuse to allow weaker nations to take measures to protect their own vulnerable economies. In this way, the economic superpowers ensure that less advantaged nations' resources, wealth, and markets remain at the full disposal of corrupt, exploitative cartels and transnational corporations with their already tested schemes to plunder and monopolize the assets and resources of defenseless peoples.

It should be clear, then, that globalism and globalization are not the same; on the contrary, they are polar opposites. Globalism gives rise to communication, peace among individuals and societies, brotherhood, compassion, and the fair sharing of benefits and resources. Globalization, by contrast, arises from, and gives rise to groundless self-importance, hegemony, control, exploitation, greed, global conflicts of all sorts – be they cultural, economic or, military – and a 'globalistic' regime that is imperialistic, monopolistic, and unjust.

Together with the growth of the communication movement – which has broken down more and more of the temporal and geographical barriers that once separated the peoples of the world and the global exchange of interests on land and on sea, in the air and in space, physically, electronically, and with and without wires – the globalistic, scientific phase of human development, which commenced with the message brought through the Prophet Muhammad, has moved the peoples of the world closer to becoming a single global community. Moreover, whereas a single global community and government may at one time have seemed a mere pipe dream, the globalism movement afoot today has rendered such notions far more realistic.

Thinkers and reformers need to be aware of the fact that the current movement toward a truly humane globalism is an experiment of tremendous significance whose failure would constitute a painful, nay, catastrophic loss to humanity, and whose success would represent the fulfillment of a long-cherished dream. It would be no less than the achievement of the purpose for which human beings have been made God's stewards on earth: namely, a life founded on brotherhood, justice, peace, and prosperity.

Communication, mutual recognition, and shared interests among the world's nations and peoples will propel them toward the formation of a single human community, which reflects the oneness of their origins and interests, and their pristine, God-given aspirations. A single human community would, by nature, be subject to a single governmental order and shared, harmonious values that give rise to peaceful relations among members of the society. In such a situation, the individual is subject to the law, and relations based on power and violence are disavowed except in cases in which the legally ruling authority is required to act in order to rein in those who defy the order of the society and violate the rights of its members. The existence of international organizations such as the United Nations, despite their observable flaws and failures, is one sign pointing to the establishment of a humane, harmonious global order.

The critical question here is: will the nature of this single society, order, and government be determined by the globalizing forces of modern-day society, ruled as it is by a materialistic, racist, exploitative capitalism? Will they be determined by an order in which the strong dominate the weak, in which might is right? So, will humanity find itself in a jungle of 'creative' chaos, odious bigotry, and monopolies of power and wealth? Will it slip anew into the abyss of devastating conflicts – the first fruits of which have begun to appear in the form of endless revolutions and wars all over the world which, be they wars of self-interest, resistance, or terrorism, are outcome of tyranny, hegemony, and exploitation on the part of the modern-day pharaohs and pseudo-prophets of materialism?

The other alternative is that of globalism – that is, the establishment of a global community, order, and government on the basis of the principles of brotherhood, justice, cooperation, solidarity, security, peace, and a responsible, constructive use of freedom. This type of freedom protects the rights and interests of both the individual and the society, its limits being defined through a process of consultation that includes all strata of the society ("...Verily, the noblest of you in the sight of God is the one who is most deeply conscious of Him" *sūrah al-Ḥujurāt*, 49:13). What this means, in essence, is that the Muslim community has the responsibility to regain its vision and base its consultative system on a perspective whose point of departure is the fundamental unity of humankind. Viewing the spheres of human experience in terms of interlocking circles, this perspective affirms human diversity on both the individual and the communal levels; this is the essence of the Qur'anic worldview and the final divinely revealed message to human beings.

Reform must begin by rescuing the Muslim community from the distortions and falsehoods to which it has fallen prey and by creating a model of the global society whose scientific, inclusive perspective was conceived in the womb of the Muslim community. This model was first established during the days of the Prophet as a challenge and a beacon of hope both for present-day Muslims and humanity as a whole.

God Almighty says:

> This [message] is no less than a reminder to all mankind – to every one of you who wills to walk a straight way. (*sūrah al-Takwīr*, 81:27–28)

> Call thou [all mankind] unto thy Sustainer's path with wisdom and goodly exhortation, and argue with them in the most kindly manner:... (*sūrah al-Naḥl*, 16:125)

> O mankind! Be conscious of your Sustainer, who has created you out of one living entity, and out of it created its mate, and out of the two spread abroad a multitude of men and women. And remain conscious of God, in whose name you demand [your rights] from one another, and of these ties of kinship. Verily, God is ever watchful over you!... (*sūrah al-Nisā'*, 4:1)

Peace

As the Almighty Source of peace and compassion, God has given us the Qur'anic worldview as a guide by means of which to apply the principles of justice and establish the unity of mankind. Peace is based on the fact that, as we have already mentioned, humanity consists of diversity in unity, and unity in diversity. That is to say, humanity is a complex entity, which manifests itself in interpenetrating circles that begin with the individual and extend outward to the whole of the human race:

> ...do good [unto others] as God has done good unto thee; and seek not to spread corruption on earth: for, verily, God does not love the spreaders of corruption! (*sūrah al-Qaṣaṣ*, 28:77)

> ...but rather help one another in furthering virtue and God-consciousness, and do not help one another in furthering evil and enmity;... (*sūrah al-Mā'idah*, 5:2)

> God is He save whom there is no deity: the Sovereign Supreme, the Holy, the One with whom all salvation rests,... (*sūrah al-Ḥashr*, 59:23)

> ...God invites [man] unto the abode of peace, and guides him that wills [to be guided] onto a straight way. (*sūrah Yūnus*, 10:25)

> But if they incline to peace, incline thou to it as well, and place thy trust in God: verily, He alone is All-Hearing, All-Knowing! (*sūrah al-Anfāl*, 8:61)

> O you who have attained to faith! Surrender yourselves wholly unto God, [literally, "Enter fully into peace..."] ... (*sūrah al-Baqarah*, 2:208)

These selections from the Qur'an are some of the most important principles of Islamic thought, all of which could be further subdivided and analyzed, thereby yielding still more principles and criteria on the basis of which to detail the Islamic scientific method, the purpose of which is to establish a righteous, sound, healthy society.

Reform and Construction

It is part of people's God-given nature to strive to obtain what they need in life. However, in the course of our striving for life and survival, there are opposing forces at work within us. On one hand, there is an animal-like tendency to prey on others and to obtain what we need by force if necessary. After all, *al-nafs al-ammārah bi al-sū'* (the self that incites to evil) is ready and willing to respond to its needs by resorting to force, violence, injustice, and aggression. On the other hand, there is a healthy, altruistic force within us that manifests itself as a spiritual awareness and a sense of what is right that moves the individual to act in accordance with the values of truth, justice, and compassion. As we are reminded by the following words from the Qur'an:

> For, unto him who shall have transgressed the bounds of what is right, and preferred the life of this world [to the good of his soul], that blazing fire will truly be the goal! But unto him who shall have stood in fear of his Sustainer's Presence, and held back his inner self from base desires, paradise will truly be the goal! (*sūrah al-Nāziᶜāt*, 79:37–40)

Khālid ibn Miᶜdān related that the Messenger of God had said, "The best food one could possibly eat is that which he has earned by the sweat of his brow. Indeed, the Prophet David, may peace be upon him, earned his own keep."[9] Similarly, ᶜĀ'ishah said, "The work of which the Messenger of God most approved was that in which a person perseveres."[10] Al-Ṭabarānī relates in *al-Awsaṭ* that the Prophet said, "If you undertake some task, God wants you to do it to the best of your ability." He also said, "Human beings are like unto God's family. Hence, those most beloved to Him are those who are the best to their family."[11] Similar to this is the Prophet's statement that:

> "Those most beloved to God are those who most help others, and the work most beloved to God is to bring joy to a Muslim's heart, to relieve him of some distress, to perform some religious duty on his behalf [should he die before being able to do so], or to prevent him from suffering hunger..."[12]

Anas ibn Mālik tells us that the Messenger of God once said, "If, when the Day of Judgment is imminent, one of you has a palm seedling in his hand, then if he is able to plant it before the Hour arrives, let him do so."[13]

Human beings' God-given ability to perceive the purposefulness and ethical core of existence and the link between the cosmos and the Creator who brought it into being likewise enables them to see the overall features of their role as stewards of God on earth. This same ability imbues people with an awareness of their responsibility to make good use of their freedom of choice, including the duty to put the earth's resources to constructive, compassionate use, while holding the forces of corruption, injustice, and aggression at bay.

The divine revelation reflects our God-given human nature and affirms the centrality of morals, conscience, and an understanding of life's mysteries and laws. Similarly, it affirms our God-given ability to develop the earth in creative ways, thereby establishing the value of constructive work well done and its role in enabling us to be the stewards we were meant to be and, in so doing, realizing the meaning of human existence and achieving true self-realization. When the Qur'anic worldview serves as our foundation, this sense of responsibility guides our stewardship and our decision making in such a way that we help by living in accord with its ethical principles to fulfill the purposes for which the creation was brought into being. In this way, we help to ensure that our endeavors to meet our material and spiritual needs take the form of righteous action and work well done in a spirit of accountability, humility, and fairness.

The eternal life of the world to come is simply an extension or reflection of the quality of life we have led in this world, whether through conscientious striving, beneficial, constructive action, reform, development, wholesome enjoyment and the peace and tranquility these bring – or through striving propelled by greed, selfish ambition, and corrupt desires and the anxiety, confusion, and regret these leave in their wake. As we are reminded by the divine revelation:

> ...Whatever good deed you send ahead for your own selves, you shall find it with God: behold, God sees all that you do. (*sūrah al-Baqarah*, 2:110)

> Yea, indeed: everyone who surrenders his whole being unto God, and is a doer of good withal, shall have his reward with his Sustainer; and all such need have no fear, and neither shall they grieve. (*sūrah al-Baqarah*, 2:112)

Beauty: Reality or Illusion?

Of relevance to the concept of reform and construction is the value of beauty in the Qur'anic worldview. Beauty is a universal value, which is manifested in the grandeur and masterful precision of the visible cosmos. Moreover, the human psyche has an inborn need for beauty and the pleasure it brings in all areas of life, both physical and spiritual. Moreover, just as beauty permeates all aspects of the observable universe (*al-manẓūr*), so also does it permeate the written revelation (*al-masṭūr*) through its descriptions of the wonders of the creation and the blessings God has bestowed on humankind, blessings by means of which we receive enjoyment and satisfaction through the senses of hearing and sight.

Regrettably, however, the rhetoric of self-negation that has prevailed for so long in Islamic discourse has suppressed the opposing discourse of self-realization, and in so doing, has gradually extinguished Muslims' ability to enjoy the beauty of creativity, the mastery of an art, and the wonders of harmony, symmetry, and complementarity to be experienced in, for example, a masterfully done painting or an exquisite piece of music. Consequently, Muslims for the most part no longer strive with confidence and peace of mind to develop their creative aesthetic capacities. Instead, they experience a needless struggle within themselves between their God-given desire and need for beauty on one hand, and on the other hand, the conviction that by indulging such a desire, they are engaging in something forbidden or sinful. This, in turn, serves further to dull their consciences and undermine their ability to distinguish between right and wrong, between refreshment and debauchery. All this, moreover, is the outcome of an illusion, namely, the illusion that in the context of meeting our innate needs, there is a conflict between the message of the divine revelation (*al-masṭūr*) and the realities of the world of sensory perception (*al-manẓūr*).

It is flaws such as these in the prevailing Muslim mentality which have produced atomistic, literalistic thinking and a disregard for the factors of time and place that are so significant for the proper application of Islamic principles and concepts to changing circumstances, conditions, potentials, and challenges. Moreover, this same tendency toward atomistic, literalistic thinking has enabled political leaders and organizations to employ the 'scholarly' in the service of political power and control over the affairs of the Muslim community, by which means they subject the interests of the community as a whole to the interests of a small minority. Over time, despotism, oppression, and corruption have extinguished the flame of stewardship and constructive engagement and the concomitant values of beauty, creativity, and self-sacrifice. This, in turn, has made it possible for those in power to advance and preserve their own vested interests through a deceitful misuse of the example represented by the generation of Muslims who lived in the days of the Prophet. That is, by appealing to examples of the wars of self-defense and resistance which the early Muslims were obliged to wage against hostile Arab Bedouin tribes and aggressive nearby empires, such leaders have kept their populations locked into a warfare mentality that leaves no room for recreation, creativity, or aesthetic enjoyment. Together with the rhetoric of subjection and self-negation, this contrived perspective has enabled autocratic rulers to repress vital aspects of our God-given nature, while furthering terrorism and political oppression.

Thus it is that Muslims have failed to appreciate much of the significance and value of beauty as it is portrayed in the texts of the Qur'an and the Prophetic Sunnah. Such texts convey the aesthetic dimensions of existence through a variety of images and rhetorical styles, and through descriptions of the creation in its beauty and grandeur. The pursuit of beauty and its enjoyment are inseparable from the full experience of self-realization, which is a natural extension of the God-given human nature affirmed in the Qur'an. Nevertheless, this affirmation of the human need for beauty – or any other human need, for that matter – must not be understood to mean that the changing realities of time and place, which for a variety of reasons (social, spiritual, cultural, and the like) may not reflect human nature in its healthy state, are what alone determines the proper applications of Islamic teachings or the most suitable way to meet human needs.

Hence, it behooves Muslim thinkers and leaders to read both the Qur'an and the important texts to be found in the Prophetic Sunnah with a comprehensive point of view – by means of which they can penetrate to the true meanings of both the Qur'an and the Sunnah as both pertain to the significance and role of creativity, harmony, symmetry, and beauty in the life of the individual and the community. Despite the lack of clarity among Muslims at this time concerning what the Islamic worldview has to say about our innate love of beauty in the various spheres of existence, we find that gleams of light from the Islamic worldview within the Muslim mind and heart have led to the most exquisite creativity in various areas of enjoyment, both auditory and visual; these areas include the recitation of the Qur'an, the singing of hymns and religious songs, calligraphy, and Islamic architecture and ornamentation.

Of significance is the fact that the Messenger of God – despite the challenges he faced in his day – affirmed the importance of enjoyment and recreation, since weariness leads to boredom and lethargy. We read in *al-Muᶜjam al-Awsaṭ* that the Supporters (*al-anṣār*) of the Prophet once wanted to join in a wedding celebration, but some of the Prophet's Companions objected to the idea. The Prophet's response was to tell these Companions not to interfere. In so doing, he demonstrated his appreciation for the human need for recreation, entertainment, and the enjoyment of the beauties of singing and dancing. In fact, he went so far as to compose a festive, even witty wedding song for the occasion, to be sung to the beating of drums. Similarly, we find that the Messenger of God made it possible for his wife, the Mother of the Faithful ᶜĀ'ishah, to enjoy watching a troupe of Abyssinian men who had come to Madinah to dance and put on a display of strength and skill with their spears and shields (*Ṣaḥīḥ Muslim*).

The Islamic worldview does not promote deprivation for the sake of deprivation: we are not required as Muslims to deprive the eye of the pleasure of seeing, the ear of the pleasure of hearing, nor the imagination of the pleasure of creativity and beauty; any such belief is based on a misunderstanding of certain passages from the Qur'an or the Prophetic Sunnah having to do with visual representation and sculpture (two-dimensional and three-dimensional art) – associated with pagan, polytheistic worship or the use of music in gatherings devoted to drunkenness and debauchery. For these represent instances of seeing and hearing that have nothing to do with the experience of beauty, but rather with decadence, perversion, and excess – in short, with those worldly pursuits to which the Qur'an refers as "...an enjoyment of self-delusion..." (*sūrah Āl ᶜImrān*, 3:185).

God Almighty says:

> He has created the heavens and the earth in accordance with [an inner] truth, and has formed you – and formed you so well; and with Him is your journey's end. (*sūrah al-Taghābun*, 64:3)

> O children of Adam! Beautify yourselves for every act of worship, and eat and drink [freely], but do not waste: verily, He does not love the wasteful! Say: "Who is there to forbid the beauty which God has brought forth for His creatures, and the good things from among the means of sustenance?" Say, "They are [lawful] in the life of this world unto all who have attained to faith – to be theirs alone on Resurrection Day...." (*sūrah al-Aᶜrāf*, 7:31-32)

> And the earth – We have spread it out wide, and placed on it mountains firm, and caused [life] of every kind to grow on it in a balanced manner. (*sūrah al-Ḥijr*, 15:19)

> ...the two great bodies of water [on earth] are not alike, the one sweet, thirst-allaying, pleasant to drink, and the other salty and bitter: and yet, from either of them do you eat fresh meat, and [from either] you take gems which you may wear; and on either thou canst see ships ploughing through the waves, so that you might [be able to] go forth in quest of some of His bounty, and thus have cause to be grateful. (*sūrah Fāṭir*, 35:12)

> And He creates cattle: you derive warmth from them, and [various other] uses; and from them you obtain food; and you find beauty in them when you drive them home in the evenings and when you take them out to pasture in the mornings. And they carry your loads to [many] a place which [otherwise] you would be unable to reach without great hardship to yourselves. Verily, your Sustainer is most compassionate, a dispenser of grace! (*sūrah al-Naḥl*, 16:5–8)

> For it is He who has brought into being gardens – [both] the cultivated ones and those growing wild – and the date-palm, and fields bearing multiform produce, and the olive tree, and the pomegranate: [all] resembling one another and yet so different!... (*sūrah al-Aʿrāf*, 6:141)

> And indeed, We have set up in the heavens great constellations, and endowed them with beauty for all to behold; (*sūrah al-Ḥijr*, 15:16)

> Behold, We have adorned the skies nearest to the earth with the beauty of stars, (*sūrah al-Ṣāffāt*, 37:6)

> Do they not look at the sky above them – how We have built it and made it beautiful and free of all faults? (*sūrah Qāf*, 50:6)

> Behold, We have willed that all beauty on earth be a means by which We put men to a test, [showing] which of them are best in conduct. (*sūrah al-Kahf*, 18:7)

> [And God will say:] "O you servants of Mine! No fear need you have today, and neither shall you grieve – [O you] who have attained to faith in Our messages and have surrendered your own selves unto Us! Enter paradise, you and your spouses, with happiness blest!" [And there] they will be waited upon with trays and goblets of gold; and there will be found all that the souls might desire, and [all that] the eyes might delight in. And therein shall you abide.... (*sūrah al-Zukhruf*, 43:68–71)

In an account related earlier on the authority of ʿAbd Allāh ibn Masʿūd, we are told that the Messenger of God once said, "No one shall enter paradise in whose heart there is even so much as an atom's weight of conceit." Upon hearing this, one man said, "But one generally likes his clothing and shoes to be nice-looking." In reply the Messenger of God said, "Indeed, God is Beautiful and loves beauty. As for conceit, it is wanton disregard for the truth and contempt for others."[14] The same message is conveyed by the following hadiths:

> Abū al-Dardā' related that the Messenger of God had said, "If you come to visit your brethren, dress your very best and put your saddlebags in order. Thus will you distinguish yourselves among people. Verily, God does not condone obscenity/indecency [*al-fuḥsh*] and ...."[15]

> Abū Hurayrah related that the Prophet had once said, "God-given human nature (*fitra*) is manifested in five things: circumcision, shaving the pubic hair, clipping the nails, plucking the hair under the armpits, and clipping the moustache;"[16] "Verily, God loves to see the effects of His generosity on His servant,"[17] and, "If anyone has hair, he should take good care of it."[18]

> Once, when the wife of Ibn Abī al-Ṣaqr was visiting ʿĀ'ishah, the Mother of the Faithful, she heard a woman ask her, "O Mother of the Faithful, I have hairs on my face. Shall I pluck them out in order to look more beautiful for my husband?" ʿĀ'ishah replied, "Yes, remove whatever would detract from your appearance, and prepare to meet your husband the way you would if you were preparing to make a visit. If your husband instructs you to do something, comply with his wishes, and if he insists that something be done, honor his request. And take care not to receive into your house someone he disapproves of."[19]

> Abū Darr related that the Messenger of God had said, "The best thing with which to conceal gray hair is henna or *katam*."[20]

It will be clear from the foregoing that when beauty is cultivated in response to sound impulses (such as the desire to please one's husband, to honor someone one is visiting, and the like), it brings satisfaction and contentment in both this world and the next; when, on the other hand, it is cultivated in pursuit of purely worldly aims or illicit pleasure, it becomes 'an enjoyment of self-delusion.'

CHAPTER III

THE QUR'ANIC WORLDVIEW: THE FOUNDATION, STARTING POINT, AND INSPIRATION FOR REFORM AND CONSTRUCTION

IN order for us as Muslims to recover our Qur'anic worldview, we will need to become more fully aware of our history as a nation, and in particular, the era spanning the lifetime of the Prophet and that of the rightly guided caliphs. We need to appreciate the effect of the Qur'anic worldview on that enlightened era, on the Islamic heritage, and on the course of subsequent eras, which in turn left their mark on the history of the entire human civilization, culminating in the current phase of scientific, cosmic awareness.

At the same time, we need to realize, in light of the Qur'anic worldview, the true meaning and essence of contemporary materialistic Western civilization, a civilization which has abandoned religion and the guidance of divine revelation for reasons having to do with its particular religions' histories and heritages and the state in which these religions find themselves now. For the message these religions brought, having been tailored to the circumstances and cultural development of the people to whom it was addressed, has now fulfilled its purpose. Given the transition humanity has made to a new era of scientific, global thinking and awareness, and due to the distortions that have turned these religions into something on the order of superstitious rites, they have become increasingly marginalized in the West, and accordingly, have come to exercise less and less influence over Western societies. As a consequence, Western civilization has adopted a materialistic orientation which has instilled in it the same lifeless, amoral qualities of matter itself. In short, the materialistic philosophy that permeates Western civilization has given rise to a kind of jungle ethic – which manifests itself in a bigoted devotion to one's own race or national group, an inclination to prey on others, dominance and control by the strong, and the absence of moral restraint in relating to others.

On the one hand, in light of what we know about the spiritual worldview founded on justice and the brotherhood of all – and on the other, the materialistic worldview founded on racism and aggression – we can begin to discern the true features of the jungle that parades as modern civilization. Such features are discernible despite the idealistic claims with which much of this civilization's conduct and policies are associated – policies which, for the most part, reflect the degree to which this civilization has departed from a lost spiritual ideal. Today's world continues to move at an exponential rate in the direction of nationalism, racial superiority, selfish interests, and bigoted disdain for or hostility toward the foreigner and whoever or whatever is different or 'other.' Hence, one can see that the sweet talk of such governments and their media outlets about ideals, human rights, and the like are little more than a predator's ruses and a facade for Machiavellian policies and designs.

Hence, the features we observe in modern civilization are, in reality, concrete expressions of the law of the jungle and the propensities of the self that incites to evil. For 'nationalism' and 'citizenship' in modern states and societies play a role parallel to that of the solidarity exhibited in the jungle by members of one species or line over against all others. However, as the foundational structures of such societies grow increasingly rigid and fragile, the societies themselves begin to weaken and disintegrate. For power politics are in perfect keeping with the inclination toward conflict among the various species and lines in the wild, where the law of might is right rules the day, and where the strong has the right to prey on the weak. In relations governed by the law of the jungle, there is no place for the pursuit of truth, justice, and fairness in dealing with one's fellow human beings, nor is any consideration given to the need to adhere to ethical standards or ideals if such standards conflict with the gains one might be able to secure by flouting them. In short, neither ethics nor rights have any meaning or place in the world of the jungle. Hence, this civilization will not be able to survive because the ongoing conflicts that arise inevitably from the foundations on which it stands are like a blazing fire, which if it finds nothing else to consume, will consume itself:

> And, indeed, after having exhorted [man], We laid it down in all the books of divine wisdom that My righteous servants shall inherit the earth: herein, behold, there is a message for people who [truly] worship God. (*sūrah al-Anbiyā'*, 21:105–106)

> Say, "Go all over the earth and behold what happened in the end to those [who were thus] lost in sin." (*sūrah al-Naml*, 27:69)

> Now there is a kind of man whose views on the life of this world may please thee greatly, and [the more so as] he cites God as witness to what is in his heart and is, moreover, exceedingly skillful in argument. But whenever he prevails, he goes about the earth spreading corruption and destroying [man's] tilth and progeny: and God does not love corruption. (*sūrah al-Baqarah*, 2:204–205)

As for the conscientious spirituality embodied in *al-nafs al-lawwāmah* (the accusing voice of man's own conscience), it finds perfect expression in the words of the Qur'an, which God has pledged to preserve from all distortion or corruption. For, contrary to the selfish propensities to which a decadent materialistic philosophy panders, the divinely revealed messages uphold the highest ethical standards and the values of truth and justice in human relationships and dealings. The materialistic, covetous mindset to which divine revelation stands opposed is reflected in the words of Iblīs who, having been commanded to bow down to Adam, said, "...Shall I prostrate myself before one whom Thou hast created out of clay?" (*sūrah al-Isrā'*, 17:61), and, "...I am better than he: Thou hast created me out of fire, whereas him Thou hast created out of clay" (*sūrah al-Aʿrāf*, 7:12). Indeed, given the free will with which they have been graced, human beings have possessed the capacity for evil from the time they were created. It was with this awareness that before Adam's creation, the angels protested, saying to God, "...Wilt Thou place on it such as will spread corruption thereon and shed blood...?" (*sūrah al-Baqarah*, 2:30).

The conscientious spirituality upheld by the Qur'an, which embodies a commitment to justice, tolerance, and ethical purposefulness, is the polar opposite of such degenerate materialism. The Qur'an urges believers to commit themselves to what is just and right, "...even though it be against your own selves or your parents and kinsfolk...." (*sūrah al-Nisā'*, 4:135), and "...even though it were [for the sake of] a near kinsman;..." (*sūrah al-Mā'idah*, 5:106). Similarly, we read:

> ...never let hatred of anyone lead you into the sin of deviating from justice. Be just: this is closest to being God-conscious. And remain conscious of God: verily, God is aware of all that you do. (*sūrah al-Mā'idah*, 5:8)

> As for such [of the unbelievers] as do not fight against you on account of [your] faith, and neither drive you forth from your homelands, God does not forbid you to show them kindness and to behave towards them with full equity: for, verily, God loves those who act equitably. (*sūrah al-Mumtaḥinah*, 60:8)

> ...but rather help one another in furthering virtue and God-consciousness, and do not help one another in furthering evil and enmity; and remain conscious of God: for, behold, God is severe in retribution! (*sūrah al-Mā'idah*, 5:2)

> And thereupon We made you their successors on earth, so that We might behold how you act. (*sūrah Yūnus*, 10:14)

Despite its overall rejection of the guidance of revelation, modern materialistic civilization has achieved great things thanks to its commitment to the systematic, law-governed method of scientific inquiry, which constitutes one of the requirements for the task of being God's stewards and representatives on earth. Nevertheless, the base, worldly propensities that mark modern civilization and those who subscribe to it (the whims and desires of the self that incites to evil) stand in dire need of still another requirement of true stewardship – namely, the conscientious spirituality inherent in sound, rightly guided human nature, *al-nafs al-lawwāmah* (the accusing voice of man's own conscience). For without it, there will be no way to confront the perilous spiritual and social ills from which the members of modern society suffer and which have begun to reach crisis proportions. Nor will we be able to resolve the fundamental existential questions in the face of which modern Western man stands perplexed – armed as he is with nothing but his own limited logic and knowledge and with superstitious, formalistic religious ethics that have nothing to say about the universals of the cosmos and human existence.

Once Islam is correctly understood and communicated to others in an appropriate manner, once out understanding of the Qur'anic worldview is purged of distortions, and once sound educational practices are adhered to – we will be equipped to offer deliverance to modern-day materialists from the conflicts, injustices, and dangers that imperil their existence. Similarly, Islam will be recognized as the source of the guidance and wisdom for which the materialists have been longing, as well as peace of mind, prosperity, and social well-being. The task of reform belongs to Muslim thinkers and pioneers who, in order to overcome cultural restraints and rigid, backward thinking, will need a generous dose of objectivity, patience, and courage.

CHAPTER IV

THE ISLAMIC WORLDVIEW AND HUMANITARIAN ETHICAL CONCEPTS

NO observant student of Islam could fail to be aware of the rich store of humanitarian ethical concepts and values embodied in the Qur'an, the Prophetic Sunnah, and the lives of the Prophet's Companions – or the gems to be found in Islamic writings, ancient and modern alike. By the same token, however, such a student is bound to note that the reality of life and relationships to be observed in modern Islamic societies fails to reflect many of these noble concepts and ideas. The reason for this is that the thinking of the Muslim community is dominated by a kind of atavistic attachment to traditions, practices, and applications of the past, while the mentality of individual Muslims is marked by a passivity and apathy that have served to deepen the rift between the values and ideals embodied in the Islamic tradition on one hand, and the reality of Muslims' lives and relationships on the other. The unfortunate outcome of this rift is a Muslim community that is fragmented, backward, and marginalized – having relegated itself to the periphery of modern human history.

Values and concepts are clearly the tools by means of which the worldview or vision of a people or community is translated into concrete action. If such a vision becomes unclear or distorted, however, such values and concepts lose their effectiveness – since, without a clear conceptual connection to the vision that underlies the life of the community, its members lose the inspiration, motive force, and sense of purpose they need in order to act in accordance with it in their daily lives and relations with others.

Consequently, it will be necessary to identify Islamic values, principles, and concepts and trace them back to the Muslim community's foundational vision. Having done this, we will need to instill these concepts educationally in the minds and hearts of individual Muslims and apply them on the level of integrated, interactive social, political, and economic institutions. In this way, we can produce a vital, positive, effective Muslim community prepared to build civilizations and make history. It will be necessary to establish research centers, while the efforts of thinkers and scholars will need to be coordinated in such a way as to present an integrated Islamic worldview to the Muslim community in a clearly thought-out and cogent manner, which clarifies all relevant conceptualizations and sets out a plan for reform. Only in this way will we be able to build confidence in the present and renew people's hope in the future. At the same time, we need to help the Muslim community's academics, reformers, educators, and parents to become aware of their responsibilities and carry out their assigned roles, thereby enabling both themselves and their progeny to fulfill their God-given spiritual longings.

It will be clear from the foregoing that the Qur'anic worldview presents a realistic vision of existence in all areas, while providing guidance for the way in which we conduct ourselves in relation to both the laws of the cosmos and our own human nature. This vision takes as its starting point the concept of the absolute unity of the Divine Self and the corresponding principle of the unity and complementarity of the cosmos and its multitudinous components. It follows from this principle that: (1) an awareness of the brotherhood of all humanity is ingrained within each of us; (2) we have a human and social responsibility to live purposefully, morally, and constructively; and (3) the structure of both human life and the universe as a whole rests on a foundation of unity in diversity, and diversity in unity.

Another fact that becomes apparent here is that without a clear worldview or vision of existence, no human community will be able to build and develop a culture or civilization that is vital and effective. For, as we learn from the historical accounts of bygone nations that lost their flexibility and vitality, these were nations whose thought and vision had become muddled and confused and which, as a consequence, had lost sight of their goal and purpose. This loss of vision and purpose led in its turn to a disintegration of their social structure and a loss of dynamism:

> [It was they] who transgressed all bounds of equity all over their lands, and brought about great corruption therein: and therefore thy Sustainer let loose upon them a scourge of suffering: for, verily, thy Sustainer is ever on the watch! (*sūrah al-Fajr*, 89:11–14)

> such being God's way which has ever obtained in the past – and never wilt thou find any change in God's way! (*sūrah al-Fatḥ*, 48:23)

Beyond Vision: Lest We Sow the Sea

In order to help the Muslim community recover its vision, purposefulness, morality, and dynamism, we will need to undertake an earnest, objective, critical reexamination of this community's heritage and history in such a way that we are able to distinguish the good from the bad, the useful from the useless. In so doing, we must not be deterred by cultural taboos, ignorance, clamorous protestations, or material enticements. If we purge our intellectual, educational, and social spheres of weaknesses, prejudices, and distortions, we will be able to nurture an objective, Qur'anically grounded, global perspective that derives its inspiration from the wisdom embodied in the life of the Prophet and the ways in which he applied the teachings of the Qur'an to real-life situations. Having done this, we will be able to overcome the mental rigidity that has taken such a toll on Muslim society, robbing it of drive and vitality. To this end, we are called upon to instill the Qur'anic worldview in young Muslim minds, hearts, and consciences – including the love of God, the love of knowledge, the love of mastery, and a correct understanding of the concept of stewardship together with its underlying ethic and purposefulness.

How, then, are Muslim children to be raised with a Qur'anic view of themselves and the world? How are we to shape an educationally sound Islamic discourse of faith, which will nurture, rather than negate, our children's innate instinct to believe in the divine unity, to love God, and to live in accordance with the ethical principles expressed in the divine revelation? If we fail to develop such a discourse, we run the risk of continuing to form young people's characters through threat, intimidation, and a sense of superiority – the outcome being human beings who are passive, individualistic, and self-centered.

How are we to draw inspiration from the Prophet's example in such a way that Muslim children get a clear sense of his moral character, his wisdom, and the exemplar he was? How can we begin to see the Qur'an and the message of Islam flowing through the life of the Muslim community as blood flows through the veins of a living organism, transforming it into a civilization of goodness, justice, and peace? And how are we to see the effects of this civilization in time and place in the life and structures of the community? Can we cease viewing the life of the Prophet as nothing more than a series of military campaigns and begin instead to draw on its full riches so that our educational curricula reflect the true vision of the Companions, which was inspired by both the Qur'an and Prophet's example? We want to see for ourselves, and convey to our children how it was that by means of this vision, the Companions achieved self-realization in joy and sorrow, hardship and ease, even in sacrifice and martyrdom – and how, in so doing, they defended the Muslim community, their families, and their religion just as they defended human rights, honor, and dignity, yet with motives untainted by a propensity for aggression, greed, or unbridled ambition and base passions.

Knowledge and understanding are, first and foremost, the craft of thinkers, scholars, academicians, and intellectuals, as well as that of schools and teachers. The parents' tasks are, first and foremost, child-rearing and the education and refinement of their children's spirit and conscience, and guidance in their children developing proper conduct. This is not, of course, to deny the auxiliary role played by the teacher and the school; nor is it to deny the impact of the media and the social environment. However, we must beware of confusing roles and neglecting or disregarding the responsibility to be borne by both the home or the school, lest we undermine the performance of either.

With all due appreciation for the educational role and impact of the media, it must also be acknowledged that at the present time, the media consists primarily of a conglomerate of governmental and commercial institutions influenced by interests and forces over which parents have little direct control. In fact, many such institutions work at direct cross-purposes with the educational goals that parents are striving to achieve. Herein lies the importance of the educational role of the family. Children who have received a positive, healthy upbringing will frequently respond disapprovingly to nonconstructive or negative messages they receive through the media, whereas this is not the case with children who have not received such an upbringing.

If, for example, a child who has not received a morally and spiritually sound upbringing watches a television program that features an ingenious way of carrying out a crime – a burglary, for example – he may not being limited by a strong moral boundary, copy the crime given certain social factors. As for a child who has received a sound upbringing, he will most likely pay little attention to the scene, since he has no inclination toward aggression or criminal behavior. In fact, seeing such a thing on television might arouse a reaction of condemnation. However, he might also benefit from what he has seen at some point if he finds himself in a situation that requires him to get himself out of a fix, to prevent the commission of such a crime.

At the same time, of course, it should be recognized that in the absence of a strong familial and parental role in a child's upbringing, continual exposure to the commercial media with its tendentious, unwholesome, and corrupting content is bound to have a negative impact on a child's mentality and spiritual and emotional state. Families should not simply look on passively, then cast the blame on the media for the effects of their own negligence, since it is the family, and the mother in particular, that lays the foundation for a child's basic way of thinking and feeling. This way of thinking and feeling in turn constitutes the prism through which children see and understand events, then translate them into concepts and values which govern their actions and their manner of relating to others both now and in the future.

What this means is that thinkers, educators, and reformers need to pay particular attention to writings and institutions that concern themselves with research on education from a cultural, scientific perspective – and then make such research available to parents by whatever means possible, particularly now that we live in the age of electronic mail and the Internet.

Education in Islamic countries is, for the most part, represented by an 'ignorant' child squatting on the floor or seated at a desk and being dictated to by a 'teacher.' The child then memorizes what the teacher has said and repeats it back to him. The lesson consists entirely of what the teacher has to say, which is then regurgitated, digested or undigested, by the student. Education in active, responsive, productive, creative communities consists of exploration, activity, movement, and practice in workshops and laboratories, libraries, playing fields and tournaments, and on trips to places of relevance to what is being taught and learned, while the curricula used include not only books, but in addition, models, presentations, documentaries, illustrated materials, and discussions.

In short, education among those participating in more innovative education has long been a matter of thought, movement, and action. In other words, life among them is a matter of action, building, and creativity. As for the education of most people, it has long been a matter of the tedious repetition of words and phrases, many of which are little more than rhetorical bluster uttered by 'leaders' into the ears of 'followers' – by those in command (the petty pharaohs) into the ears of obsequious, hypocritical subordinates, and by semi-ignorant 'teachers' into the ears of miserable, persecuted, 'ignorant' learners. (I say this with sincere apologies to those teachers who themselves have been victims of the educational system in Islamic countries, and who have been poorly trained, poorly paid, and ill-treated both professionally and socially.) Consequently, it comes as no surprise to find that life within the Muslim community has become synonymous with empty words, empty dreams, and empty hopes – while among others, it is synonymous with action, searching, investigation, development, the use of resources, mastery, and creativity. "O you who have attained to faith! Why do you say one thing and do another? Most loathsome is it in the sight of God that you say what you do not do!" (*surah al-Ṣaff,* 61:2–3.) Accordingly, the individual in the society whose educational system is sound and interactive becomes a source of productivity, power, and wealth – while, in our present society, he becomes a recipient of unemployment, weakness, and poverty.

Hence, if thinkers and reformers are serious about sowing the earth and not the sea, as it were, so as to help the Muslim community to recover its strength, drive, and constructive, creative potential as a steward of God's gifts, they have no choice but to work patiently and diligently to reform, purify, and renew their culture, a process that will require the reform of their educational curricula and methods of child-rearing – and the recovery of their original Qur'anic vision of themselves and the world.

When we have begun at last to concern ourselves with thought, knowledge, with understanding and the university, with the workshop, with the school, and with parental nurture as part of the educational process; when we have enriched our cities, neighborhoods, and towns with libraries, our languages and cultures with translations that broaden our horizons and increase our knowledge, our institutions with expertise, experience, and competence, and our factories with skilled labor; when we have freed our thinking from the shackles of inertia and our relationships from anachronistic strictures that have robbed the Muslim community of its creative impetus; when the family, the school, the workshop, and the factory have become the object of care and concern – in other words, when the individual human being in all his or her potential and creativity receives the nurture and encouragement he or she needs in order to become a fully contributing, honored member of Muslim society, then, and then only, will we know that we are living out the Qur'anic worldview. Then, and then only, will we know that thinkers, leaders, reformers, educators, academics, and parents have successfully fulfilled their respective roles, and that the wheel of Islamic civilization has begun to turn once more. Then, and then only, will Islam and the Muslim community occupy a position of honor and strength – providing guidance for human individuals and societies, lifting high the banner of mutual consultation, justice, brotherhood, and peace, and dispelling the dark clouds of backwardness, injustice, tyranny, and corruption.

If, on that day, the Muslim community anywhere in the world finds itself in need of more skilled professionals, they will come without hesitation. As things are now, however, our religious, social, and educational institutions are headed exclusively by those who have exhibited poor performance in their respective fields – while, in the meantime, we reserve our resources and recognition for those fields that we expect to be lucrative and prestigious, such as medicine and engineering. However, given the poor performance of our social system, we eventually lose the very physicians and engineers on whose training the Muslim community had spent long years and exorbitant sums because of their decision to leave their homelands and their community of faith and travel to the ends of the earth in search of a decent wage and a life of dignity. If we truly honored our thinkers, educators, scholars, physicians, engineers, and others who perform such services for their communities with the proper preparation and professional consideration, they would not leave their homelands in search of a better life elsewhere, and if we needed more individuals with skills like theirs, we would have enough and more of them available to us.

Nevertheless, we should not underestimate the importance of means and methods, be they material or otherwise, and whether they pertain to education, training, or preparation. After all, they are a necessary expression of human nature, the laws of the cosmos, and the Qur'anic worldview alike. At the same time, however, such means and methods need to be in good hands – that is, in the hands of people who are effective, active, and competent mentally, psychologically, spiritually, and doctrinally, and hence conscientious and diligent concerning the manner in which they are used and developed.

The time has come for all of us to take our lives with the seriousness they deserve, and to base the life of our Muslim community on the Qur'anic perspective on human beings and the world in which they live. It is time for us to purify and rebuild our culture and provide our children with the proper spiritual, intellectual, and cultural foundation. In this way, Muslims will be able to achieve self-realization, understand the meaning of their existences, and be able to be a blessing to themselves, their family, and their community.

How Do We Develop Islamic Social Sciences and Live Out the Islamic Vision?

Before bringing this work to a close, I would like to devote a discussion to the issue of developing the Islamic social sciences by means of which we will generate sound Islamic thought. There has been a good deal of controversy and confusion over the true nature of 'the Islamization of knowledge' and the way in which it is to be achieved. One of the most important reasons for this is the lack of clarity with which the issue of developing the Islamic social sciences is presented, as well as the failure to clarify the nature of their content and purpose and how they are related to the Islamic heritage, Islamic thought, and the Western social sciences, respectively.

Consequently, this issue needs to be presented clearly and straightforwardly in all its fundamental details to students of both traditional Islamic studies and the Western social sciences. The reason for this is that the Islamization of knowledge and the Islamization of the social sciences are two sides of a single coin, and until we can clarify the link between them, as well as the link between them and the traditional Islamic sciences or disciplines and the social sciences, confusion will continue to reign and the currently ongoing 'dialogue of the deaf' over the meaning and nature of the Islamization of knowledge, as well as the action plan required to bring it about, will see no end.

In order to overcome this ambiguity, we need to define the nature of the traditional scholastic Islamic sciences as they are engaged in at the present time, as well as their uses and their programs of study. Additionally, we need to determine the nature of contemporary social sciences, both secular and Islamic, as well as the way in which they are studied and the functions they perform in contemporary life. Lastly, we need to identify the methodological and ideational relationship between contemporary Islamic social sciences and both the Islamic heritage and modern Western social sciences on the level of sources, ideational content, and study and research methods.

Let us begin, then, with an examination of the issue of thought and the traditional Islamic sciences, that is, the traditional mode of examining the Islamic heritage, on the level of content, function, and the role such sciences play in the life of the Muslim community. Not surprisingly, the juristic (legal) aspect of the Islamic tradition receives the greatest emphasis in Islamic thought as it pertains to the life of the Muslim community. The role of jurisprudence in the life of human societies is to translate the community's doctrines, unchanging principles, and values into laws, legal rulings, and judgments which govern and order the life of the society and the relationships among its members and institutions.

Islamic jurisprudence has, from its inception, derived its thought and content from the examples set by the Prophet and the rightly guided caliphs, including the arrangements, practices, and applications that marked the life of the Prophet and the lives of the Companions who governed the Muslim community after his death. With the termination of the rightly guided caliphate and the era of the Companions' rule,[1] things deteriorated to the point where the sacredness of the city of Madinah itself was attacked, with the catastrophic result that the scholars representing that school were banished from the public sphere. Thus, began the scholastic era in which Islamic thought proper was relegated solely to the sphere of the mosque, personal status laws, and private, individual dealings and affairs.[2]

The conditions that had prevailed during the days of the Prophet and the rightly guided caliphs remained essentially unchanged for quite a while – and the examples set by the Prophet and the rightly guided caliphs in their arrangements and the details established at this time – remained the ideal models for the ongoing life of the Muslim community. Indeed, the precedents established by the Prophet, his Companions, and the rightly guided caliphs constituted the most important source of scholastic Islamic thought. However, with the passage of time and the growing isolation, which was imposed upon religious scholars and the religious tradition, such scholars exhibited a tendency to go overboard in recording the texts of the Prophetic Sunnah, both those which were well-attested and those which were not – thereby resorting to subjugation through the appeal to sanctity and the rhetoric of intimidation as a means of concealing their political and intellectual impotence.

The ongoing ideational and political isolation and powerlessness suffered by students of the Islamic legal sciences led, over time, to a worsening intellectual rigidity and inertia that manifested itself in the practice of relying on literalistic rules, regulations, and precepts derived from practices, arrangements, and conditions many of which were no longer of any relevance to later Islamic societies. This, moreover, is precisely the situation we are facing in Muslim societies today, whose circumstances, store of knowledge, potentials, and challenges differ radically from those of the eras in which Islamic juristic rulings were originally derived. What this means is that many Islamic laws, regulations, rulings, and legal decisions are tailored to conditions and challenges other than those that are relevant to the age in which we live. In other words, despite what the Islamic heritage embodies by way of lofty principles and values of direct relevance to the realities that obtained in the days in which their original applications were derived, many of the applications and legal opinions based on such principles are linked to a historical reality that no longer exists. As a result, they belong to an era that is past, and not to the reality being lived by the Muslim community today.

It is vital that the unchanging principles and values of the Islamic worldview be recognized and preserved, because the Muslim community is in greater need of them today than it ever has been. The ways in which the Prophet and the rightly guided caliphs applied the Qur'anic vision and its underlying principles to the circumstances they faced constitute a treasure trove of wisdom and understanding for us, who stand in dire need of the guidance they have to offer us in our own day and age. By allowing ourselves to benefit from this undying wisdom, we generate new dynamism within the sphere of Islamic thought, and are better able to perceive what concrete steps are called for in order to respond appropriately to the needs of the Muslim community as it seeks to nurture healthy, sound relationships among its members and to build the effective institutions needed in order to face the challenges of contemporary life.

As for the link between modern Western social sciences and the Islamization of knowledge – a link that lies at the heart of the Islamic social sciences – it has to do with both content and method. However, if we deal separately with content and method, we will get a clearer picture of things and be able to deal with them more easily and fruitfully. Before embarking on this discussion, it will be important to clarify the function of the social sciences in the field of knowledge and social relationships.

In order to ascertain the function of the social sciences, we will need to be aware as a matter of principle that the social role and function of the social sciences differ from those of law, jurisprudence, and legal rulings and decisions. The function of the social sciences is essentially that of studying society in light of its cultural vision, be it spiritual or material, within the parameters of its human and material potentials and the cultural challenges of the time period defined by the study. In short, the function of the social sciences in any society is to generate social change and stability in the various areas of life – the political, the economic, and social – and on the individual, institutional, and communal levels alike.

In an Islamic society in particular, the social sciences provide the ideational content from which law and juristic research derive the rules and regulations that order relations among the society's members and its institutional structures. In other words, the function of jurisprudence and the law is, first and foremost, formal in nature, while the function of the social sciences is primarily intellectual or ideational. As a result, they complement one another by working together to promote the progress of the Muslim community and its civilization.

The question that now arises is: what is the link between contemporary Western social sciences and the issue of the Islamization of knowledge and the development of the Islamic social sciences? In this connection, it is important to draw a distinction between Western thought generated by sociological research and study, and the methodology employed in the Western social sciences. Based on such a distinction, we see that the development of the Islamic social sciences is not opposed to past tradition. On the contrary, such development can draw on the experience, expertise, and achievements of the past, while at the same time drawing on the methodology and achievements of the Western social sciences.

The ideational content of the Western social sciences is influenced by two factors. The first factor is the subjective, ideological element that manifests itself in the Western worldview, which is essentially a materialistic ideological perspective. Hence, religion no longer plays any appreciable part in the vision, dealings, or social relations of Western peoples, many of whose members look upon themselves as agnostics. As for the second factor, it is the objective element represented by the research methods employed in the Western social sciences, whose object of study is human nature and its manifestations, including the ways in which people interact with their environment and the ways in which their psychological energies and human propensities can be put to use toward the fulfillment of this vision and its associated aims.

The objective aspect of the ideational content of the Western social sciences – which has yielded numerous creative tools, systems, and institutions – can be drawn upon and benefited from in the development of the Islamic social sciences. At this point, someone might ask: by benefiting from the notion of studying human nature and the laws that govern individual and communal behavior, including the material influences that operate on human beings, have we become dependent on the West, and are we 'importing' something foreign to our Islamic worldview?

This question can be answered unequivocally in the negative. For Islam came in order to renew the human civilizations that existed at the time of its appearance – some of which, like the Persian empire, were civilizations that had served their purpose and grown aged, weak, unproductive, and corrupt, and others of which, like ancient Greek civilization, had gone bankrupt and come to a complete end. With Islam, there dawned a new era that opened up the horizons of a global, scientific manner of relating to the universe, and which promoted knowledge, wisdom, prudence, learning, creative thought, research, and investigation. Islamic civilization inaugurated an era of scientific research and the study of the laws and patterns of the universe at a time when the then – West of the dark ages knew nothing of such things. Rather, the West acquired such disciplines from schools and universities established by Muslims, from its contact with the Muslim community, and from the translations of Muslim scholars' writings into European languages.

The Western social sciences with their associated research into human nature and its social expressions are simply an extension of the study of the laws and patterns of the cosmos on the material level. They have helped to generate social thought, which has served as the basis for the development of institutions of various kinds, as well as the legal thought needed to manage Western societies' affairs in keeping with their materialist understanding of themselves and the cosmos. However, the world continues to suffer the ill effects of such a materialist view of human nature and the cosmos due to its dualistic values and standards, which have led to the woes of colonialism, injustice, war, and destruction.

Of all the peoples on earth, Muslims would have been the best qualified to lead the way in the scientific study of human nature and the divinely established laws and patterns of the created world. However, the errors into which the Muslim community fell early in its history have had long-lasting effects, thereby impeding its progress and depriving humanity for long centuries of the guidance offered by Islam and the divine revelation.

What we can conclude from the foregoing is that Muslim students and researchers need to do the following four things: (1) free themselves from the habit of imitation and mental subordination, arming themselves with a creative, comprehensive, critical, scientific, and analytical way of thinking; (2) develop a good understanding of the Qur'anic perspective on human beings and the world around them, with its unchanging values and principles; (3) equip themselves with a thorough knowledge of the scientific method of studying human nature and the laws and patterns of the material universe, as well as human societies and their potentials and strengths within the context of their particular temporal and geographic contexts; and (4) benefit from both the Islamic heritage and the scientific achievements of modern Western society so that, with a knowledge of these, they can explore the horizons of human potential and the universe, and create the means to enable human beings to make genuine improvements in the world around them and to achieve 'the good life' in both this world and the next.

It should be noted in this connection that the IIIT has taken a number of significant steps in the area of academic research, which offer a model for scholars in the area of Islamic studies, social studies, and methodological studies, as well a model for academic research centers and universities. By studying, emulating, and developing this model, we may help to shift the focus of current efforts from mere outward forms and rhetorical one-upmanship to the service of what genuinely matters – namely, the Islamic worldview with its unchanging values and concepts.

There is a need for the publication of reference works in the area of Islamic methodology and its academic sources, and for training programs for academicians and thinkers in this field. As an important initial step toward the formation of a sound contemporary Muslim perspective and mature Muslim intellectuals and academics, Islamic universities can establish a double major consisting of simultaneous specializations in Islamic studies and sociology. This step has in fact been taken by the IIIT in the Islamic and Social Studies Program at the International Islamic University, Malaysia (IIUM), where it has proved a notable success worthy of replication and development.

The IIIT intends over the coming years to expend greater effort in the area of writing and academic training in the methodology of the Islamic social sciences. In this manner, it hopes to highlight issues pertinent to the Islamic vision generally and, more specifically, to the values and principles at the heart of this vision as they apply to real-life situations and challenges. It is hoped that support for these efforts will be forthcoming from thinkers, reformers, and academicians, as well as from institutions of higher education and academic research centers.

CHAPTER V

THE INTERNATIONAL INSTITUTE OF ISLAMIC THOUGHT'S PLAN FOR THE DEVELOPMENT OF UNIVERSITY CURRICULA

THE IIIT has contributed to the reform of university curricula through a model being implemented at the International Islamic University, Malaysia (IIUM). This model consists of a double major – or, rather, a major specialization and a minor specialization in the faculties of Islamic revelation and the humanities respectively. One of a student's two specializations will be in Islamic studies; then, if the student chooses to complete a secondary specialization, or minor, by extending his studies for an additional year (thirty or forty credit hours), he or she will receive two bachelor's degrees, one in Islamic studies, and the other in an area of the humanities or social sciences.

This system, which has met with considerable success, is turning out graduates who are highly competent in their respective areas of specialization, who have a clear sense of their Muslim identity, and who exhibit considerable maturity – and an understanding and appreciation of the Islamic worldview and the Muslim community's role in the progress of human civilization. As a means of further developing this model, a comprehensive reform plan has been drawn up for the university curriculum, and a selected group of university professors specializing in Islamic studies have been assigned the task of setting out the details of the plan and specifying its academic content.

The backbone of this plan is a general course of study in Islamic studies that consists of two parts. The first part (approximately thirty credit hours) provides the student with what a Muslim needs to know about his or her religion – that is, the doctrines, principles, values, concepts, aims, and rites that serve as the foundation for a fully rounded Islamic perspective and a principled, goal-oriented character. This part constitutes a required minor specialization for every student majoring in religious studies, social studies, or the humanities. As for the second part (also around thirty credit hours), its aim is to impart general knowledge of the history of the Muslim community, the life of the Prophet, the Islamic civilization, and the traditional religious (Islamic) sciences.

In addition to this general curriculum in Islamic studies, there are two other types of courses. The first of these are courses in social sciences and the humanities, and the second type consists of specialized courses in the religious sciences. The latter courses include Islamic law and jurisprudence, doctrine and philosophy (*ʿilm uṣūl al-dīn*), the hadith sciences (*ʿilm al-ḥadīth*), Qur'anic exegesis (*ʿilm al-tafsīr*), the biography of the Prophet (*ʿilm al-sīrah*), Arabic grammar (*ʿilm al-naḥw*), and rhetoric (*ʿilm al-balāghah*).

Note should be made here of a syllabus that has been developed for a critical, analytical, conceptual study of contemporary Western materialist civilization and its underlying ways of thinking, as well as the various dimensions of its relationship to and influence upon the Muslim community. This course of study has been established as a partial specialization at IIUM under the title, 'Occidental Studies,' or, 'Studies in Western Thought and Culture.' The purpose of this course of study is to turn out experts in the understanding of Western culture who, as a result of such expertise, are able to relate effectively to the positive aspects of this culture without falling prey to its negative aspects. IIUM also provides courses that support the remaining specializations in this respect. We hope to see this partial specialization developed into a full major, which would meet a great need among professionals within the Muslim community.

In sum, each student's degree program will consist of two specializations, the first part of which is the Islamic studies curriculum (the backbone). This first part is an inseparable component of every student's study program regardless of what his or her other specialization or major happens to be (social sciences, humanities, legal studies, economics, or religious studies), and whether this other specialization is primary (his or her 'major') or secondary (his or her 'minor'). Hence, every student's bachelor's program will be one of the following:

> 30 hours of Islamic studies + 60 hours of major subjects + 30 hours of auxiliary coursework = a 120–130 hour degree program in one of the social sciences, humanities, or religious specializations.
> 60 hours of Islamic studies + 30 hours of minor subjects + 30 hours of auxiliary coursework = a 120 hour degree program in Islamic studies.
> 60 hours of Islamic studies + 30 hours of a specialization in education + 30 hours of auxiliary coursework = a 120–130 hour degree program in Islamic studies, which qualifies one to teach the fundamentals of Islam on the primary and secondary educational levels.

If a student completes a minor specialization in such a way that it becomes a major specialization, the graduate will, in effect, have two bachelor's degrees: one of them in Islamic studies, and the other in his or her other area of specialization.

It should also be noted that there are approximately 30 hours of auxiliary coursework for one's 60-hour major, which brings the total number of hours required for graduation with a bachelor's degree in any specialization to 120–130 credit hours, while the hours required for a double major comes to 150–170 hours. The breakdown of credit hours is as follows:

> 60 hours (major specialization) + 30 hours (minor specialization) + 30 hours (auxiliary coursework) = 120–130 hours (bachelor's degree).
> 120 hours (bachelor's degree) + 30 hours (minor specialization) + 30 hours (completion of a minor specialization such that it becomes a major specialization) = 150–180 hours (a double major, which is the equivalent of two bachelor's degrees).

It is important to note that the core content of many one-semester courses can be covered in two credit hours only rather than three, particularly in the second part of the Islamic studies curriculum.

The auxiliary coursework for specializations in religious studies must cover the broader social aspects of the subject matter being treated, thereby broadening students' horizons and helping them to understand the psychological dimensions of whatever their specialization happens to be from a practical, realistic perspective. It is also important that the auxiliary coursework include three comprehensive introductions to three areas of psychosocial study. In addition, the courses entitled, 'The Family and Parenthood' and 'Creative Thinking and Problem-Solving' must be required of all students without exception. If possible, it would also be good for the course entitled, 'The Rise and Fall of Civilizations' to be a requirement for students specializing in religious studies, the social sciences, and the humanities, since Islam arose in a region that gave birth to a number of civilizations that prospered and declined in succession. Moreover, these civilizations have left their distinctive marks, both positive and negative, not only in this region, but on the cultural identities and characteristics of the peoples who belong to the Muslim community worldwide.

The details of these curricula were finalized during the 2008–2009 academic year, and it is hoped that they will be a source of benefit to other programs of higher education throughout the Islamic world. As for the question of how the scientific facts now available to humanity and the new potentials that now exist can be employed in the service of the Islamic worldview in the areas of the social sciences, the humanities, the physical sciences, and technological applications – its answer will be the fruit of the accumulated scientific research that has been done, and which continues to be done, in many of these fields. Thanks to the efforts of IIIT academic teams working to bring about the unification and Islamization of knowledge, such research has also begun to yield academic treatises on methodology.

As for the physical and technical sciences, it is preferable, given the extensive and demanding nature of their requirements, that they have a program that includes the major part of the first section of the Islamic studies curriculum together with an overview of the cultural dimensions and mission of the Muslim community. In addition, such a program should contain auxiliary coursework on the philosophy of Islam as it pertains to these sciences and the aims that guide their use in real-life, practical situations, particularly those aspects that pertain to each student's specific specialization or major. Then, if there are students who wish to know more about Islam as both a religion and a civilization, they are free to seek out more information on these topics. It is for this reason that IIUM offers diplomas, master's degrees, and doctorates in Islamic studies to any graduate of any academic specialization once he or she has completed the requirements for his or her initial specialization. In addition, a student specializing in the physical sciences may take Islamic studies as a second specialization if he or she so chooses.

A Flexible Program

Lastly, it should be noted that this plan is highly flexible, and can therefore be adapted to a variety of university plans and to the requirements of different specializations. Since sixty hours are the minimum requirement for any major specialization, this leaves thirty to forty hours for auxiliary coursework. Up to twenty hours of auxiliary coursework can be added to any major specialization, thus bringing the number of hours up to eighty, which is the maximum allowed for any specialization, while the remaining ten to twenty hours are reserved for other university requirements and auxiliary coursework. In this manner, then, students are prepared for post-university life by being given an integrated, well-rounded education encompassing at once the academic, the emotional, the spiritual, and the cultural. As a consequence, they are better equipped to fulfill the constructive, reformist mission of Islam.

The task before us, then, is clear and simple, and if the intention to renew and reform ourselves is sincere, our hopes are bound to be fulfilled, God willing.

Educational Curricula and Programs

I have discussed in considerable detail the subject of education in my work entitled, '*Azmat al-Idārah wa al-Wijdān al-Muslim,*' where I seek to make clear that the human being's inward makeup is determined not only by reason and knowledge, but equally importantly, by upbringing and spiritual-emotional factors. I also stress the fact that a child's upbringing is, first and foremost, the responsibility of the family. Consequently, I have a longstanding interest in writings addressed to parents, and this has become one area of interest for the IIIT. Nevertheless, schools and the universities have a vital educational role to play, not only by conveying knowledge, but in addition, by instilling discipline in students' performance, behavior, and relations with others based on an objective, practical perspective of themselves and the world around them.

It is with this responsibility in mind that the IIUM's curriculum includes a course on the family and childrearing, as well as one on creative thinking and problem-solving, the purpose of which is to prepare students for the challenges of the future – and particularly, their role as parents. It is hoped that through the education young people receive at IIUM, they will see the importance of raising their children in an egalitarian atmosphere that promotes courage, inward integrity, critical thinking, initiative, and creativity. In this way, such young people may help to counter the authoritarian approach to child-rearing that is far too prevalent in the Muslim community today, and which generates a 'slave mentality' and the tendency to obey others out of fear and blind subservience rather than genuine respect and conviction.

For this same reason, the study plan developed at the IIUM aims to promote a culture of debate and discussion throughout the entire student body. The goal of this policy is to train students in their capacity as future citizens, thinkers, and leaders in the ability to understand and appreciate others' points of view, mentalities, motives, and aims. And in fact, the IIUM has succeeded in promoting flexibility, good communication skills, tolerance, and humility – qualities which leave no room for one-sided thinking and viewpoints or the bigoted, closed-minded attitudes that provide fertile ground for the growth of totalitarianism, cruelty, and corruption. IIUM's graduates have thus acquired invaluable social and leadership skills, which are evident in their performance and in their way of relating to others, while IIUM debate teams have achieved outstanding success on both the local and international levels.

In sum, effective, successful education is not merely a process of spoon feeding or memorization, but is rather first and foremost a process of developing abilities and skills while creating a social and academic atmosphere that exposes students to a variety of academic and practical experiences and skills. It is this same type of atmosphere that the IIIT strives to produce in the area of Islamic thought and university education through its various academic and educational publications. To this end, the IIIT presents practical models that can enable educational institutions to achieve better performance and thereby play an effective role in improving the conditions of the Muslim community.

A Final Word

In conclusion, I would like to draw the attention of university professors, thinkers, writers, and researchers to the fact that many of their writings contain terms and treat concepts of relevance to issues of vital importance to the Muslim community. However, until such concepts and terms are translated into concrete action plans, programs, systems, and mechanisms that challenge, reform, and refine the Muslim community's way of life, they will remain nothing but literary flourishes that have no effect in the real world in which we live.

It is to be hoped that the efforts of Muslim thinkers, reformers, academicians, and other concerned specialists will be coordinated in such a way that they give the Muslim community both a clear vision and a guide to action so that it can correct its way of thinking, revitalize its institutions, make good use of its potentials, and give free rein to its creative energies. Otherwise, the Muslim community will remain in the grip of mental indolence, subordination, and dependency.

I have attempted in the foregoing to apply basic Islamic values and concepts to actual situations faced by the Muslim community and to provide both conceptual and practical alternatives to current practices and ways of thinking. In so doing – in the service of the Islamic vision for human civilization and the planet – I have sought to provide models that can be expanded upon and adapted as needed by both thinkers and practitioners, each of them according to his or her field of specialization. "And in the morning,[1] the people will rejoice that they broke camp before the break of dawn."

In God do we seek assistance, and on Him do we rely.
He is the Best of all protectors, and the Best of all helpers.
Praise be to God, the Lord and Cherisher of the worlds.

APPENDIX I

EQUATIONS FOR REFORM

The following six equations may be seen as mnemonic devices that serve to remind us of the major issues that have been discussed in this volume and what the contemporary Islamic reform effort requires:

Equation 1:
Revelation + awareness of human nature and the laws of the cosmos + reason + time + place = scientific, rightly guided Islamic knowledge and a sound intellectual approach.

Equation 2:
An upbringing consisting of love + encouragement + freedom + discipline = a positive, effective, constructive, strong human character.

Equation 3:
A Qur'anic perspective on human culture + convictions inspired by monotheistic faith = a human being with a constructive, positive, ethically sound will and the desire to act creatively and responsibly as God's steward and representative on earth.

Equation 4:
A sound intellectual method + a positive spiritual and emotional orientation + the will to do good = self-realization based on the Qur'anic worldview embraced and applied by the Prophet's Companions.

Equation 5:
Thinkers + educators + reformers + an effective worldview = genuine, peaceful change.

Equation 6:
A constructive, positive vision + a sound intellectual method + a sound educational method + effective social institutions + social and economic justice = a vital, egalitarian, spiritual, creative, dynamic, effective, capable, constructive society and culture.

Appendix I

The Basic Foundation for the Structure of Islamic Civilization

A Spiritual, Constructive, Stewardship-based, Monotheistic Worldview

↓

A Positive, Scientific, Intellectually Coherent Approach
(the School and the Media)

↓

A Positive Spiritual and Emotional Upbringing (the Family)
An Effective, Humane Social and Institutional Structure (the State)

↓

A Society of Peace, Freedom, Justice, Harmony, and Brotherhood
(the Wider Muslim Community)

↓

A Human Civilization Marked by the Pursuit of Knowledge, Globalism, and
Relationships Governed by Justice, Compassion, Freedom, and Peace. [1]

From Here We Begin to Teach and Learn:
The Requirements of Cultural Construction

A Human Civilization Marked by the Pursuit of Knowledge, Globalism, and
Relationships Governed by Justice, Compassion, Freedom, and Peace.

↑

A Society of Peace, Freedom, Justice, Harmony, and Brotherhood
(the Wider Muslim Community)

↑

An Effective, Humane, Social and Institutional Structure (the State)

↑

A Positive Spiritual, and Emotional Upbringing (the Family)

↑

A Positive, Scientific, Intellectually Coherent Approach
(the School and the Media)

↑

A Human Civilization Marked by the Pursuit of Knowledge, Globalism, and
Relationships Governed by Justice, Compassion, Freedom, and Peace.

From Here We Begin to Teach and Learn

APPENDIX II

FAITH: A MATTER OF REASON, OR THE MIRACULOUS?

Introduction

The reason I have chosen to append this essay to a discussion of the Qur'anic worldview is that it presents the infrastructure required by this worldview in its capacity as a global spiritual vision having to do with the universals of existence and human life on earth in all its dimensions. After all, no comprehensive vision of life and what lies beyond it will have any authoritative basis unless it issues from the Creator of the universe, since an understanding of the universals of existence cannot be based on human reason alone.

The purpose of this essay is to clarify the logical, theoretical foundation for faith, which in turn constitutes the foundation upon which the Islamic worldview rests. A reasoned faith has served, whether consciously or unconsciously, as the underpinning and guiding light for my own life since the time when I was a young child, giving meaning to my existence on the material and spiritual levels alike. My hope is that what I have to say here will help Muslim readers discern the solid foundation they have for their own faith, and that, in so perceiving, they will see the meaning of their own lives and form a clear worldview based on faith in the oneness of God and their own role on earth as God's stewards, representatives, and reformers.

In the course of studying the issue of the Islamic scientific method some years ago, my attention was drawn to the fact that, despite the scientific bent and disciplined nature of the philosophical system developed by Imam Ibn Ḥazm al-Andalusī (d. 456/1064), he nevertheless departed from his own logical, scientific method – when in treating the issue of faith and the authoritative nature of revelation, he resorted to an acceptance of the miraculous and supernatural.

As a boy I came face to face with questions relating to faith, the religious worldview, and the truthfulness of the revelation. In coming to grips with these issues, my thinking tended in the direction of the logical and the rational. Hence, the miraculous played virtually no part in the way in which these issues were resolved for me. It was with these thoughts in mind that I felt prompted some years ago to write an article entitled, 'Reflections on the Literalism of Ibn Ḥazm and the Inimitability of the Muhammadan Message'[1], in which I raise a number of questions relating to Ibn Ḥazm's method and offer ways in which his scientific and methodological vision might be filled in or completed.

Rational Proof as the Best Foundation for the Authoritative Claims of Revelation

Ibn Ḥazm is a prominent figure in the history of Islamic philosophy and theology, who was known for his scientific, systematic, and disciplined manner of thought. Adhering strictly to the criteria of reason, realism, and sensory data and experience, Ibn Ḥazm was eminently bold and clear in both his arguments and his conclusions. As such, he rejected empty conjecture and delusion even if they happened to parade as solid religious or intellectual notions. Indeed, Ibn Ḥazm's scientific, systematic approach was itself one of the most important reasons for the loss of favor he suffered when, as time went on, the thinking of the Muslim community lost its proper focus, and its thinkers and scholars became increasingly isolated from the concrete, practical aspects of the community's life.

Ibn Ḥazm's adherence to the literal sense of the text of the Islamic revelation in the derivation of Islamic legal rulings is a natural extension of his scientific methodology, which relies solely upon reason, sense perception, and concrete experience. Hence, pertaining to the realm beyond immediate sense perception or human logic, Ibn Ḥazm's approach does not allow human beings either to add to or subtract from that which is revealed directly by God. In Ibn Ḥazm's belief, human reason is obliged to understand the revelation exactly as it is, without addition or subtraction, since to do otherwise – that is, to mix the world of reason and sense perception with the realm that goes beyond them without any authoritative or rational justification – leads either to the deification of human reason or to its abolition.

Ibn Ḥazm employed his reason, his knowledge, and his scientific method in the understanding of the Islamic revelation and its texts without adding to it or taking anything away from it. As a result of this disciplined approach, he formulated a system of jurisprudence that commanded the respect of his supporters and detractors alike. Indeed, his writings came to be viewed as a source of legitimate, authoritative arguments which seekers of knowledge and understanding continue to draw upon to this day.

Proponents of the systematic, scientific approach have often been disregarded by Muslim scholars, and this to the detriment of the Muslim community and its intellectual progress. The vitality, dynamism, and adaptability of Islamic thought have been sapped by the failure to integrate knowledge from life's various spheres and the insistence on confining the work of Muslim scholars and intellectuals to the realm of the mosque or school. This lack of recognition, appreciation, and welcome has been the fate not only of Ibn Ḥazm, but of many other creative thinkers and proponents of the scientific approach as well. Such thinkers include Imam Ibn Taymiyyah (d. 729/1328), who incurred the enmity of numerous Muslim scholars and intellectuals and was accused of disloyalty to the Islamic religion, as well as the renowned Ibn Khaldūn, whose thought and writings were ignored or received with indifference by the majority of Muslim scholars until Western, non-Muslim proponents of the scientific approach brought his writings to light and granted them the recognition and appreciation they deserve. And other examples abound.

Whoever reflects on the lives of these rare geniuses, who lived after the door to ijtihad[2] was shut at the close of the fourth century AH, will discover that these thinkers were adhering to an approach that differed in both quality and trajectory from the prevailing school-based intellectual models, in which knowledge remained fragmented and scholars remained isolated from the currents of day-to-day life. Ibn Taymiyyah, Ibn Ḥazm, Ibn Khaldūn, and others of their kind were not scholars and jurists who did their work in isolation from the realities being experienced by the society around them. On the contrary, they were men who had acquired expertise, wisdom, and awareness through concrete practice in the social and political spheres on the basis of which they had developed an integrated, scientific mindset. Their knowledge was of the sort that related clearly to their action, their practice, and their awareness in such a way that they dealt authentically with life's changing realities. Hence, when viewed in relation to the conditions of the age in which they lived, most of their opinions and interpretations may be seen to have been valid, realistic, and enlightened.

However, despite the reliability of Ibn Ḥazm's scientific method and the disciplined manner in which it deals with the realms of the seen (*al-shahādah*) and the unseen (*al-ghayb*), it nevertheless comes up against a major difficulty in its search for the rational evidence required in order for someone to accept the notion of divine revelation as a source of knowledge and, on this basis, to accept and adhere to Islamic law. For, given the fact that Ibn Ḥazm was committed to the authority of reason and empirical evidence and, on this basis, rejected Gnostic, mystical, and esoteric claims, he was obliged to identify a kind of systematic, scientific, rational evidence upon which he could rely in his acceptance of and commitment to divine revelation (*al-ghayb*).

A reasoned acceptance of the authority of divine revelation requires a prior acceptance of the veracity and trustworthiness of the Apostle, as well as the veracity of the message he brought. At this point, however, we find Ibn Ḥazm to be torn between his scientific, rational method – which will accept nothing other than reason and sense experience as legitimate sources of knowledge – and his personal faith in the grandeur of the message of Islam, as well as its necessity for the harmonious flow and integrity of human life, and the need for the realms of the seen and the unseen to meet, as it were, and complete one another. For this reason, Ibn Ḥazm had no choice but to go in search of a kind of rational evidence, which would be consistent with the nature of his thought and method, and which would, thereby, constitute a credible link between the realms of the seen and the unseen.

Since it would have been impossible for someone of his persuasion to accept claims of the possibility of Gnostic (mystical) communication or communion with the world of the unseen, Ibn Ḥazm had to turn to the life of the Messenger of God for the evidence he sought as the basis for a rational, scientific belief in his truthfulness. The truthfulness of the Apostle would have to have been manifested through living proof of the sort that would leave reason no choice but to believe his claims and surrender to this belief. The existence of something extraordinary (*al-iʿjāz*) in the life of the Apostle would serve as a rational, scientific basis for acceptance of and surrender to his message in the realm of the rational and the sensory (*al-shahādah*). Moreover, it was through this acceptance that the rational link between the realms of the rational and sensory, on one hand, and the suprarational and metasensory (metaphysical), on the other, would be brought to completion. This logical, systematic point of departure is, by necessity, the only sound one within the parameters of Ibn Ḥazm's scientific, rational approach to claims pertaining to the suprarational and the metaphysical.

The question then arises: what miraculous or extraordinary dimension of the Prophet's life could Ibn Ḥazm appeal to as that which compels rational acceptance of the truthfulness of his message, leaving no room for doubt or dispute?

It may be seen here that despite the fundamental soundness of Ibn Ḥazm's method, he nevertheless missed the mark by failing to derive the correct conclusions based on the premises he had posited and to which he had committed himself. For the extraordinary element which Ibn Ḥazm identified in the life of the Prophet consisted in the miracles he is reported to have performed in the physical realm. The problem we face here is that even if believers find it easy to affirm that these miracles took place, there nevertheless remains room for a great deal of controversy on the rational or scientific plane concerning the soundness of the chains of narrators who related these events, the soundness of the accounts themselves, whether the narrators exaggerated or embellished their accounts, the matter of whether the senses might have been deceived, and so on. Considerations such as these might even lead us to conclude that the only people who are required to believe that these miracles took place are those who witnessed them directly. Hence, if some people affirm their occurrence based on a predisposition to grant the truthfulness of such claims – out of love, reverence, and admiration for the person to whom they are attributed, or out of love and respect for the scholars who affirm that they occurred or who accept these accounts simply to avoid 'rocking the boat' – the fact remains that such an affirmation is inconsistent with Ibn Ḥazm's rational, scientific method.

I, like Ibn Ḥazm, have scientific, rational inclinations. From the time I was a secondary school student in Makkah not far from the Holy Kaᶜbah, I became aware of issues surrounding the relationship between the world of reason and sensory perception on one hand, and the world of the suprarational and metaphysical on the other, as well as the question of which direction to take in life and what doctrines to believe in and commit myself to. Thanks to our family's well-stocked library and a loving, nurturing family environment that encouraged my academic leanings from an early age, it came naturally to me to approach such existential questions by directing my attention to the life of the Prophet. It was there that I hoped to find the missing link that would demonstrate the reliability of his claim to be conveying truths from the world of the suprarational and metaphysical, thereby commanding acceptance of and commitment to the sanctity of the message he brought, while at the same time allowing one to feel admiration and appreciation for bearers of other messages to the extent that their thought and exemplary lives merited such.

Unlike Ibn Ḥazm, however, I did not go in search of definitive proof of the Prophet's reliability and veracity in the supernatural feats he was reported to have performed in the material realm (despite my willingness to believe that he did, in fact, perform them). Rather, I turned in my search to the person of the Prophet himself. The reason for this was the realization that I could not, with my reason alone, understand existence and what lies beyond it, nor could I ask God directly about the true nature of the Apostle and his message. Therefore, it was necessary for me, logically speaking, to search for the missing link I sought in the life of the Apostle himself on the basis of the claims of reason and the God-given need for understanding without needing to bypass these claims, violate them, or declare them invalid by appealing to supernatural acts in which the laws of the universe are contravened. Even at that relatively early age, I succeeded in arriving at rational, scientific corroboration of the veracity of the Apostle without needing to believe that he had performed miracles. And it was this that inspired me to write this critique in the hope of shedding further light on rational, scientific methodology, while at the same time, pointing to the need to recover the humane, spiritual worldview of Islam in the face of the materialistic, dog-eat-dog worldview that prevails in today's world – so that, ultimately, 'right' will be 'might' rather than 'might' being 'right.'

Ever since those days of my adolescence, I have realized that the scientific method requires that the truthfulness of the final message brought by the Apostle be demonstrated in a rational, scientific manner that will enable succeeding generations to believe in it with no less certainty than that experienced by those who were contemporaries of the Apostle himself. For this reason, this *iʿjāz* (extraordinary something) unique to the Prophet must be consistent with the rules of logic and the laws of the universe for which his message demonstrated such deep respect and to which it calls us to adhere. Support for the Prophet's message and mission must not be dependent on a supernatural event or events that surpass the capacity of the mind to explain and which do not require the scientific researcher to appeal to the known laws and patterns of the cosmos. Moreover, because the basis for the message's reliability has to be related to the person of the Apostle, it is important first to examine his actions and his words – both their individual elements and their overall patterns – and then to compare them to those of others in order to see how, logically speaking, it was possible for this human being both to bring others the message of the world beyond the senses, and to lead them to believe it.

The message of Islam can be seen to have differed from the messages and religions that preceded it. For history itself has preserved for us both the text of the Islamic message and the details of the Prophet's life; similarly, both history and the text of the Qur'an make clear that Muhammad was a human being who lived a human life, and that his life was that of an upright individual. Consequently, the extraordinary element in his message and the evidence of its veracity must be consistent with the facts of the human nature to which the Islamic discourse – a discourse whose purpose is to set human beings on a course that will lead them into a phase of scientific globalism – was and is addressed. But the question remains: what was the extraordinary element in this human being's life? And where is the indisputable evidence of his truthfulness as an apostle who brings a rationally binding message of goodness from the unseen?

The message that was brought by the Prophet Muhammad as embodied in the Qur'an fulfills the two fundamental criteria for any message that can rightly be considered to have a divine origin. The first of these two conditions is that of documentation. Unlike the texts associated with the other religions of the world, the Qur'an is thoroughly documented. That is to say, the Qur'an was committed to writing during the days of the Apostle, and continues to be recited by specially qualified reciters based on fully authenticated chains of authority that are traceable back to the Prophet himself. In addition, it is required of Muslims throughout the world to recite some portion of the Qur'anic text no fewer than five times a day in the daily prescribed prayers, while the majority of Muslims voluntarily read it, recite it, memorize it, learn from it, base their daily devotions thereon, and seek blessing through it throughout their lives – a fact that affords it a level of documentation that is unparalleled among the ancient manuscripts of the world. Even more amazing is the fact that this extraordinary documentation is associated with a text that emerged among an essentially unlettered people, who had never been known for their sciences, knowledge, philosophy or advanced civilization.

As for the second condition, it might be termed simply 'goodness.' That is to say, the Qur'an exhorts its readers and hearers to pursue goodness through righteous action in the world; if it did not, there would certainly be no reason to consider it a sacred text from the Creator of life and the cosmos. Indeed, the verse that reads, "Behold, God enjoins justice, and the doing of good, and generosity towards [one's] fellow-men; and He forbids all that is shameful and all that runs counter to reason, as well as envy; [and] He exhorts you [repeatedly] so that you might bear [all this] in mind" (*sūrah al-Naḥl*, 16:90) epitomizes the Qur'anic message as a whole.

However, although documentation and teaching that exhort to goodness are necessary conditions for a message to be considered of divine origin, these alone are not sufficient to rule out the possibility that this document was created by someone as a means of self-aggrandizement. Consequently, a third condition must also be satisfied. This third condition must – by demonstrating a rational, scientific inimitability, if you will – establish indisputable proof that Muhammad was a genuine apostle who was delivering a message from God Himself, the Seer of the unseen.

Herein, then, lies the importance of engaging in a rational examination of the character of the Apostle and the details of his life, whence we can expect to derive the proof we seek of his truthfulness and the truthfulness of his message. Indeed, how could we approach the issue in any other way, knowing as we do that the message he brought is rational and scientific in nature? After all, it opens with the command to 'Read!'; it comes to us in the form of a book that encourages us to seek knowledge, to think, to reflect, and to go in search of evidence and proof; and it is based on an understanding of causes, natural patterns, and laws. All of this, again, confirms the need to examine the life of the Apostle, including his character traits, words, and actions, so as to determine what it was that qualified him to bear the message he did, and what evidence there is that his message was true.

If we put both reason and knowledge to work, giving careful thought to the Apostle's words, actions, abilities, achievements, and character traits, the evidence we seek will be near at hand. Admittedly, any one of these words, actions, traits – however great or extraordinary they might have been in and of themselves – might nevertheless have been uttered, performed, or exhibited by some other human being as well. However, when we take all aspects of the Prophet's person together, it becomes clear that the extraordinary or miraculous element belongs not in the greatness of any one particular achievement, statement, or character trait alone, but rather in the fact that there were all brought together in a single man – and in the way in which they manifested themselves in this single man, in his particular circumstances, and in the context of the cultural and historical phase through which his society was passing during his lifetime.

The beauty and wonder of this type of 'miracle' lies in the fact that it does not require that the Apostle be viewed as something more than a human being, nor does its acceptance lead to the suspension of reason and human logic. Rather, it allows the message he brought to be addressed to human beings through their God-given natures and the laws of the cosmos as they understand them. This, then, might be termed 'a rational, scientific miraculousness,' and it is this which supplies the missing link between the world of the rational and sensory (*al-shahādah*) and that of the suprarational and the metaphysical (*al-ghayb*). As such, it provides indisputable scientific and rational proof of the Apostle's truthfulness and the authoritative nature of the message he brought.

In order for us to clarify what we mean by the human, scientific, rational, comprehensive 'miraculousness' in the life of the Prophet, we will need to make a quick journey through his biography, identifying his most salient character traits and the major events of his life, then bringing them together in a complete, integrated picture. In this way, it will be possible for us to see the miraculous or extraordinary – while at the same time human, scientific, and rational – element in the life and message of Prophet Muhammad. With this larger picture of the Prophet's character before us, it becomes clear why we have no need to appeal to miracles that may not be consistent with the fundamental premises of the message he brought, nor with the nature of the scientific, global phase of human and cultural development, which his message was intended to inaugurate.

* * *

The Prophet Muhammad was born in the barren Valley of Abraham in the Arabian desert. His father ʿAbd Allāh died before he was born, and his mother, Āminah, died when he was six-years-old. He was taken into the care of his grandfather, ʿAbd al-Muṭṭalib, and later, his paternal uncle, Abū Ṭālib. Although he grew up an orphan, he was not deprived of motherly love and compassion during his early years. For a period of forty years, he passed through various stages of life during which, if he had harbored worldly ambitions, he would not have been able to conceal them. Nevertheless, after he was commissioned with the message he came to bear at the age of over forty, he showed himself to have been graced with exceptional knowledge, wisdom, leadership abilities, and a pioneering spirit in response to every situation he faced. During the years prior to the reception of his call to be a Prophet – as a boy, a teenager, a youth and a full-grown man, and as a father and husband – Muhammad was known for his truthfulness, integrity, humility, and impeccable moral conduct. Indeed, it was his solid reputation, which when he was twenty-five-years-old, led one of the most noble, prudent women of his tribe – Khadījah bint Khuwaylid – to entrust him with her wealth and seek his hand in marriage.

It is noteworthy that at the age of forty, at which time the storms of youthful impulsiveness have begun to calm and the heat of physical passions have started to cool among those whose emotions and ambitions have been at their height, we find that, just when one would least expect such a development, this man begins to present himself as someone with a divine message from the world of the unseen, at once critical and benevolent, in which he calls upon both his own people and humanity at large to affirm the existence of one God alone and to live together in humility, brotherhood, tolerance, respect, religious freedom, justice, and the love of knowledge.

So serious was the claim he was making and so earthshaking the consequences for the doctrines and way of life to which they had grown accustomed, that his people – custodians of the Kaᶜbah and worshippers of idols – responded to his message with astonishment and disbelief. Amazingly, however, he succeeded in convincing them of the truth of his claim by reminding them of his trustworthiness throughout the days he had lived among them. Given these facts, how could he, after all those years from the day he was born, have lied to them, and about a matter as weighty as this? Would it have been possible for Muhammad, or any other human being for that matter, to silence himself, suppress his true abilities, and stifle his aspirations and ambitions throughout his entire life only to reveal them without forewarning at the age of forty? Would it have been possible for Muhammad, or anyone else, to force himself to be truthful and honest from the day he was born until middle age – when, in his heart of hearts, he was really a liar and an impostor in order, now that he had reached an advanced stage of his life, to induce them to believe his lies and fabrications? On the contrary, it is fair to say that no one who had lived the life of veracity and integrity for which Muhammad had been known from the time he was a boy, could have concealed the abilities that were to manifest themselves with the passage of time unless he had truly been raised and made ready for this moment by the Divine Providence. For, until the day when he received the call to prophesy in the cave of Ḥirā', he had never exhibited even the slightest ambition or leadership potential, nor did he possess any of the expertise or practical experience that would have prepared him for the astonishing things he would achieve in the days to come.

Hence, we find that the types of abilities that emerged in the life of Muhammad after the age of forty – even if they were, essentially, merely human in nature, and even if, taken individually, they would not be seen as distinctive – were, when joined in a single person, particularly in the unsophisticated environment that had formed him, a veritable 'miracle' that compels belief by the standards and criteria of human reason itself. It boggles the mind to see this unassuming, trustworthy, honest man rise up with such unanticipated strength, calling for reform in his society, despite the fact that he was an uneducated individual from an unlettered Bedouin tribe living in one of the most remote regions on earth. Nothing in his previous experience would have prepared him to come forth with eloquent speech of the sort that he did. Moreover, he persevered in his call for truth and reform despite the persecution and affliction he and his companions suffered over the years; indeed, it was the Quraysh tribe's resistance to him and their insistence on clinging to their idols and immoral practices that reinforced his and his followers' determination to spread his message and to endure their long suffering in the face of tribulation at a time when there appeared to be no light at the end of the tunnel. Even more amazing is the fact that after thirteen years of tireless proclamation in the face of unrelenting harassment, the new community of faith, having gathered all its strength, was given an opportunity for a new beginning when the tribes of Aws and Khazraj, inhabitants of the city of Yathrib (re-named Madinah when it received the Prophet Muhammad), quite unexpectedly embraced the message of Islam, pledging to obey the Apostle and to support the message he had brought.

One is astounded to think that within ten short years, Muhammad, whose childhood and upbringing are now familiar to us, managed with unparalleled success to establish an autonomous state over which he ruled wisely and ably, and which was a model of justice, tolerance, brotherhood, goodwill, and religious freedom. Indeed, in his capacity as head of state, he constructed a system of law and order, adjudicated with eloquence and discernment and led armies to victory.

Is it not a source of wonder that a single human being could have possessed all of these potentials, abilities, and ambitions without having given any indication thereof throughout his boyhood, adolescence, and manhood, even as a husband and as a father, until the age of forty, and without there having been anything in his environment or previous experience to nurture or develop such potentials? Would it actually have been possible for someone to plan so seamlessly for such a transformation over a period of forty years without letting on for a moment that he possessed such potentials and capabilities? Moreover, how could someone with little or no worldly experience have managed to take on tribal chieftains, leaders, and rulers alike – surpassing them in wisdom, planning, politics, and combat to the point where his message and the state he had established were able to bring down far-flung, powerful empires such as those of the Persians and the Byzantines – enabling the light of his message to spread within centuries throughout the entire world despite the great disparities among its peoples, tongues, and races?

The manner in which, over a period of sixty-three years, Muhammad blossomed into a human being of extraordinary leadership ability and exemplary character is the true miracle that demonstrates the truth and authority of the message he brought. It was this message that inspired the faith of the finest, most outstanding men of his tribe, who have gone down in history for their distinctive characters and abilities. These men, who had known him and tested him, having been his peers and companions from the days of their boyhood, chose to follow him and believe in him even under circumstances in which, over a period of thirteen years of persecution and suffering, there appeared to be no hope of reprieve, still less success. How, then, can someone come fourteen centuries later – at which time we know even more than we did before about the miraculous nature of the Qur'an – and claim that he knows more about Muhammad than his own companions did, or that he is more qualified to make a judgment about him that they would have been?

The structure of a human life might be likened to that of a pyramid. It begins with a broad base consisting of parental upbringing, education, training, experiences, and practice, which later lead to a peak of ability and skill in a particular area. In this way, one might become a victorious military commander, a capable head of state and politician, an eloquent, influential writer, or an industrious, creative scientist, researcher, or scholar. The life of Muhammad, however, displays the very opposite pattern. Hence, it is best likened to an inverted pyramid whose base is narrow and whose peak is broad and spacious in all areas – in wisdom, in knowledge, in political astuteness, in eloquence – in all of which he outstripped prominent leaders, sages, scholars, and men of letters alike. Another, perhaps more fitting, analogy to Muhammad's life is that of the leaves of a flower atop a supple green stem that gradually unfolds to reveal its full beauty and fragrance, after which it yields the fruit of which it is God's harbinger.

If properly received and understood, the message Muhammad brought brings peace to the mind and heart; it promotes brotherhood and compassion among human beings; and it calls them to justice, truth, goodness, and knowledge. This extraordinary message has reached us through texts passed down by groups of individuals sufficiently large and disparate that it would be impossible for them to have colluded in falsification. Moreover, it was conveyed by someone who had always been known as truthful and trustworthy and whose character had been formed in an inimitable, miraculous manner. Hence, no rational individual could help but affirm its reliability and authenticity as a message of truth from God, the one and only Creator of all. As such, it is a binding message in which the worlds of the seen and the unseen come together and complete one another, and in which the meaning of existence and the purpose of nature – both human nature and that revealed throughout the cosmos – are fully manifested.

An appreciation of this aspect of the message Muhammad brought – which is in keeping with human reason and the natural, God-given desire to understand things on a rational basis – is therefore best suited to the enlightened, scientific, rational approach advocated by Ibn Ḥazm. Similarly, it is best suited to rationally minded contemporary Muslims who, together with humanity as a whole, are freeing themselves from the shackles of illusion, error, and idle talk and progressing toward a full embrace of the scientific method.

Scientific and practical reflections such as these have given me a firm anchor for my faith in the Islamic religion as a sacred message from God. Consequently, I am a Muslim by conscious choice rather than merely by birth or geographical happenstance. I have been protected from superstition, illusion, and deception, and my feet have been planted firmly on the path of knowledge, reason, and an understanding of human nature and the laws of the cosmos. Consequently, whenever I am assailed by any doubt in connection with the message of Islam, I am able to overcome it by engaging in a systematic, scientific investigation, which enables me to see where the truth lies rather than confirming me in my doubts and hesitations.

The following is a two-step approach to the investigation of any question or doubt. The first step is to identify the nature of the problem, while the second is to examine the particulars of the Qur'anic text in light of its universals and its overall aims and purposes. Not using this approach, in my view, leads to nothing but delusion and foolish talk of the sort that we would do best to avoid. Our instructional and investigative methods should combine knowledge of the essential aspects of our religion – including its vision, its aims, its principles, its values, and its concepts – with a solid grounding in the multidisciplinary, scientific study of human nature and the cosmos around us. For only in this way will our knowledge and practice be both effective and constructive in such a way that they serve to give concrete expression to Islam's vision, aims, principles, and values in our day-to-day lives.

Inspired by my reflections on Ibn Ḥazm's method, the vision I am proposing is based on an experience I went through as a young person. It is an experience which, whether consciously or unconsciously, every thoughtful youth will have to cope with in the process of his or her instinctual search for understanding of the relationship between the realms of the seen and the unseen. For only then can he or she find inner assurance concerning his or her final destiny.

This vision and this method have been of tremendous benefit to me over the years, and I hope they will likewise be of benefit to others by encouraging them to reflect deeply and to take life with the seriousness it deserves. Through it, I hope to have enriched our young people, who embody our dream of a better future for both the Muslim community and for humanity as a whole. This better future is one in which humanity follows the path of truth and builds a civilization of justice and brotherhood, in which we are exemplary stewards of our God-given wealth, and in which our sound understanding and our upright conduct make true self-realization possible and fulfill the meaning of life with all its responsibilities and blessings.

May the life of Ibn Ḥazm, as well as the lives of all those distinguished predecessors of ours who followed in his footsteps, provide my readers with food for thought and inspiration to commit themselves to a sound, rational approach to their faith. Then, having committed themselves to this approach, may they integrate revelation and reason in such a way that, together, they provide a guide for their lives and an inspiration to seek the good and give of themselves unstintingly by God's grace.

To God, who guides all who so desire to the path of righteousness, be praise and blessing. Praise be to God, the Lord and Cherisher of the Worlds.

NOTES

Introduction

1 Herndon, VA: IIIT, 1987; written in English in partial completion of requirements for my doctorate from the University of Pennsylvania, Philadelphia (1973). This study was later translated into Arabic by Dr. Nasir al-Burayk and published under the title '*al-Naẓariyyah al-Islāmiyyah li al-ʿAlāqāt al-Dawliyyah: Ittijāhāt Jadīdah li al-Fikr wa al-Manhajiyyah al-Islāmiyyah*'

2 The first edition of this book was edited by the late Isma'il al-Faruqi. The first revised edition in both English and Arabic was published in 1986, the same year in which Dr. Al-Faruqi was tragically murdered together with his wife Lamya in their home in Wyncote, Pennsylvania.

3 Cairo: Maktabat al-Khānjī, 1960.

Chapter I

1 *Ṣaḥīḥ Muslim*, hadith no. 6926.

2 Narrated by Aḥmad in his *Musnad*, hadith no. 18030.

3 It is important here for us to be aware of the fact that even if the universe and its laws are immutable, or nearly so, human understanding of them is a relative matter determined by factors of time and place. In other words, human beings depend for their understanding of things on the amount of knowledge available to them at a given time and place; this available knowledge might be referred to as their 'epistemological ceiling,' which will be higher or lower at one time or place than it is at another. Human beings' location in time and space, as well as disparities in their abilities and mental capacities, will impact the degree to which they are able to comprehend the realities of the universe and its natural laws. Herein lies the role of the universal principles and higher intentions made known to us through divine revelation. It is these principles and intentions that should guide human beings in dealing with their environment – regardless of the extent to which they have comprehended the facts and laws of the universe concerning which no one can attain absolute understanding or certainty. Truly did the Messenger of God speak when he said to Wābiṣah ibn Maʿbad al-Asadī, "Wābiṣah, ask yourself what righteousness and unrighteousness

are. Righteousness is whatever sets your heart and soul at rest, while unrighteousness is whatever causes unrest in your heart and soul, even if others should tell you it is right" (Narrated by Imam Aḥmad in his *Musnad*, hadith no. 18030). However, in thus consulting himself, the individual should be living out an overall vision of things that is in keeping with the God-given purposes of nature, even if he has not yet arrived at a precise scientific understanding of things. However, once one does attain such an understanding, it will be in full accord with the higher intents of both divine revelation and nature.

It was this overall perspective that was articulated by Imam Abū Ḥanīfah al-Nuʿmān, founder of the 'Opinion School' (*Ahl al-Ra'y*), who placed priority on the spirit and higher intents of the Islamic law in his legal rulings. That is to say, when the conclusions to which juristic analogies lead were not consistent with the spirit and higher intents of the law, this problem could be resolved by resorting to the practice of *istiḥsān* (juristic preference). The practice of juristic preference involves adopting the legal ruling or interpretation, which is most in keeping with the spirit – that is, the higher intents of the Islamic law for human affairs and what is known about human nature and the laws of the universe until such time as more complete knowledge calls for a change in this ruling or interpretation. Through this approach, it becomes possible to achieve a scientific, objective balance between nature and the law in specific temporal and geographical contexts.

This methological understanding of the relationship between the Islamic law and revelation on one hand, and our God-given human nature and the laws of the universe on the other, forms the basis for the theory of 'the higher intents of the law' (*maqāṣid al-sharīʿah*). However, the scholar or student applying the theory needs to be equipped with a correct knowledge of the principles of Islamic doctrine and law as well as the principles that govern human society.

The most salient textual difficulties are those that relate to certain sayings of the Prophet and our pious ancestors. Such difficulties arise in connection with the authenticity of the narrative or the precision of its wording. They may also arise due to the perceived possibility of error, corruption, or falsehood in the text. Errors in a text may have been committed unknowingly or with good intentions; however, they may have been committed out of neglect or even deliberately by those with a particular axe to grind, their intention being to lend an aura of sanctity to what they see as the correct point of view or course of action. Another reason for textual ambiguity is the modern reader's failure to take note of a specific time and geographical factors and their influence on the text's meaning. In some cases, the reader is unable to place a text in its original temporal or geographical context due to a lack of background information that would allow us to date it, or about the occasion for its having been recorded and handed down to us.

Perhaps the best known debates over such textual difficulties are those that revolve around the accounts that relate to the following: to poison, the seven dates, 'nursing' a grown man, and the wings of a fly – as well as texts relating to the realm of the unseen, the reality of magic, envy, and the evil eye, and the relationship between the world of the jinn, or invisible beings, and the world of human beings.

In the case of certain types of texts, the scientific facts presently available to us are insufficient to explain their meaning. In such cases, the need arises for a theory that will allow us to deal practically with the scientific issues the text raises. The text in question may then be explained based on certain scientific hypotheses, but not on clearly established facts. Such hypotheses provide an explanation which helps the reader relate to the phenomenon being spoken of without necessarily enabling him or her to make an unequivocal judgment as to whether the theory or its associated assumptions are correct. A salient example of such a hypothesis is Darwin's theory of the origin of species, or evolution, which presents us with a certain conceptualization of past events and a practical explanation of the resemblance and commonalities we observe between different kinds of living beings, yet without our being able to arrive at certainty concerning the correctness of this theory and its associated postulates. While, on the one hand, the vagueness of this theory is beneficial in that it allows us to accept it on a provisional basis, it also provides fertile ground for the proliferation of arbitrary philosophical inferences. One such inference, which goes hand-in-glove with materialistic philosophies, which view society as a human jungle that operates on the principles of survival of the fittest and might is right, is that the material realm is haphazard and governed by chance.

Another well-known theory of this type is that of Sigmund Freud. Freud's theories of psychoanalysis contributed to the birth of modern psychology, but have now been rendered more or less obsolete by expanded knowledge of and deeper insight into the workings of the human psyche. Still another example is the hypothesis propounded by certain modern physicists that matter can be neither created nor destroyed, and this hypothesis was later proven correct by research in the field of physics. The hypothesis of the indestructibility of matter is also useful as a way of explaining phenomena that have been observed on the subatomic level – where matter is reduced, with part of it being transformed into energy as in the case of a nuclear explosion, and where material weight increases through the transformation of energy into matter in the case of nuclear and hydrogen fusion.

Among the problems being faced by Islamic thought is the question of how far scientific research should go in the area of human genomes and stem cells given the newly developed capacity for cloning and genetic modifications. New capacities such as these open up new opportunities; at the same time, they raise critical questions: What should be allowed, and what should not be allowed? How can these various tracks of scientific research and application be regulated? What types of controls can achieve benefits for people, while protecting them from harm and even disaster? In order to address such questions, we need to agree upon and allow ourselves to be guided by the universal principles and higher aims of Islamic law – lest we succumb, on one hand, to rigid, literalistic perspectives that simply forbid everything indiscriminately or, on the other hand, to haphazard, chaotic approaches that may well open the door to catastrophe.

In sum, then, both textual difficulties and unresolved scientific issues need to be approached by means of the practice of juristic preference (*istiḥsān*) with its regard for the importance of universal principles, the underlying spirit of Islamic law, and the human interests it is intended to serve.

4 We have no record of a saying of the Prophet with this exact wording. However, we do have a saying to this effect which is attributed to ʿAlī, who said, "Speak to people based on what they know. Would you want God and His Messenger to be perceived as untruthful?" (*Saḥīḥ al-Bukhārī*, hadith no. 127). In a discussion of human reason, Abū al-Ḥasan al-Tamīmī relates on the authority of Ibn ʿAbbās [that the Messenger of God] once said, "We prophets have been sent to speak to people in a way that they can understand." However, he tells us that its chain of transmission is weak.

5 The Barmakids were a Persian family that had become quite influential under al-Mahdī. Yaḥyā ibn Khālid al-Barmakī had been responsible for Hārūn al-Rashīd's upbringing, and his wife had nursed him as a baby. Yaḥyā had been influential in bringing Hārūn al-Rashīd to the caliphate, and his sons continued in high favor until 188/803, at which time the caliph imprisoned them and confiscated their land after they had begun increasingly to take matters of state into their own hands. The result of the Barmakids' downfall was a significant reduction in the Persian role and influence over the Abbasid state.

6 In 802, the Abbasid Caliph Hārūn al-Rashīd, father of al-Ma'mūn and al-Amīn, issued instructions for al-Amīn to succeed him and for al-Ma'mūn to serve as governor of Khurasan, then succeed al-Amīn as caliph upon the latter's death. Although al-Ma'mūn was the older of the two brothers, his mother was Persian, while al-Amīn's mother was a member of the reigning Abbasid family. After Hārūn al-Rashī'd's death in 194/809, the relationship between the two brothers deteriorated. Al-Ma'mūn made moves toward independence, in response to which al-Amīn declared his own son Mūsā to be his heir. This violation of the father's will and testament led to a civil war in which al-Ma'mūn's Khurasani troops led by Ṭāhir ibn Ḥusayn defeated al-Amīn's armies and laid siege to Baghdad. In 198/813, al-Amīn was beheaded and al-Ma'mūn was recognized as caliph throughout the empire.

7 Note should be made here of the seriousness of any falsification or corruption in any sacred text or its interpretation. This applies in particular to texts of Prophetic

hadiths, since any text that is not governed by the universals of the Qur'an and the higher intents of Islamic law has the potential to severely undermine Islamic values, concepts, and aims. The effects of such a text might be likened to a drop of deadly poison that has been slipped into an otherwise wholesome meal. For however beneficial and nutritious the meal would have been otherwise and however healthy one's body might be, the tiniest drop of such poison will suffice to bring death and annihilation. A single text that allows, for example, for superstition and charlatanry could destroy the effectiveness of hundreds of authentic, sound texts – which call for adherence to the laws of the universe, whole-hearted striving for the good, mastery of one's work, integrity, and trust in God. Consequently, careful critiquing of the content of hadith narratives, be they solitary (*āḥād*) or otherwise, in light of the fundamental principles set forth in the Qur'an is a clear necessity if we are to protect the Muslim community from the falsification or misuse of certain texts and interpretations that have done so much to distort Muslim thought and doctrine and the Islamic-Qur'anic worldview.

God Almighty states:

> *Alif. Lām. Rā'.* A divine writ [is this], with messages that have been made clear in and by themselves, and have been distinctly spelled out as well – [bestowed upon you] out of the grace of One who is Wise, All-Aware... (*sūrah Hūd*, 11:1)

> ... there is no beast that walks on earth and no bird that flies on its two wings which is not [God's] creature like yourselves: no single thing have We neglected in Our decree. And once again: Unto their Sustainer shall they [all] be gathered. (*sūrah al-Anᶜām*, 6:38)

And:

> He it is who has bestowed upon thee from on high this divine writ, containing messages that are clear in and by themselves – and these are the essence of the divine writ – as well as others that are allegorical. Now those whose hearts are given to swerving from the truth go after that part of the divine writ which has been expressed in allegory, seeking out [what is bound to create] confusion, and seeking [to arrive at] its final meaning [in an arbitrary manner]; but none save God knows its final meaning. Hence, those who are deeply rooted in knowledge say: "We believe in it; the whole [of the divine writ] is from our Sustainer –albeit none takes this to heart save those who are endowed with insight." (*sūrah Āl ᶜImrān*, 3:7)

The phrase 'messages that are clear in and by themselves' (*āyātun muḥkamāt*) refers to doctrine, principles, values, concepts, and rulings – while the phrase, 'others that are allegorical' (*ukharu mutashābihāt*) refers to stories that convey moral lessons and recount events relating to the People of the Book (Jews and Christians) and peoples of bygone civilizations. In connection with such accounts, the Qur'an instructs the Muslim to be content with those found in the Qur'an itself, while leaving aside any superstitions, pagan beliefs, and misrepresentations with which they are associated.

8 Narrated by Imam Aḥmad in his *Musnad* on the authority of Qatādah, on the authority of Anas ibn Mālik, hadith no. 13991.

9 Narrated by Imam Aḥmad in his *Musnad* on the authority of Zuhrah ibn Maʿbad on the authority of his grandfather, hadith, no. 22556.

10 Narrated by Imam Aḥmad in his *Musnad*, hadith no. 25341.

11 *Ṣaḥīḥ Muslim*, The Book of Repentance, hadith no. 2747.

12 *Sunan Ibn Mājah*, The Book of Fasting, hadith no. 1690.

13 *Ṣaḥīḥ al-Bukhārī*, The Book of Marriage, hadith no. 4776.

14 *Ṣaḥīḥ al-Bukhārī*, The Book of Fasting, hadith no. 1847. It may be helpful to give attention here to an issue that has caused confusion and difficulty for many Muslim youths. The issue of which I am speaking, and which increases the sense of pressure felt by young Muslims as they find themselves carried along by the hustle and bustle of everyday life with its rapid pace and increasing demands, revolves around the need to perform the five daily ritual prayers at their specified times. In principle, of course, this necessity is a given of Muslim life: "...Verily, for all believers prayer is indeed a sacred duty linked to particular times [of day]" (*sūrah al-Nisā'*, 4:103). However, what Muslims need to be aware of is that the Prophetic Sunnah provides for a degree of latitude in this area that can significantly ease the burden they may feel in many of the circumstances they face on a regular basis. We read in *Ṣaḥīḥ al-Bukhārī* on the authority of Anas, that the Messenger of God said, "Bring ease, not hardship, announce glad tidings rather than alienating others." In keeping with this spirit, we have been allowed to join the noon prayer (*al-ẓuhr*) and the mid-afternoon prayer (*al-ʿaṣr*), as well as the sundown prayer (*al-maghrib*) and the evening prayer (*al-ʿishā'*).

The Prophet himself would sometimes combine prayers (that is, pray two prayers in immediate succession during the time period for one of the two prayers, as when one prays the noon and mid-afternoon prayers in immediate succession during the time period for the mid-afternoon prayer, or the sundown and evening prayers in immediate succession during the time period for the evening prayer) even when he had no particular extenuating circumstance, nor was he on a journey. Both *Ṣaḥīḥ Muslim* and Imam Aḥmad's *Musnad* contain the account passed down on the authority of Ibn ʿAbbās according to which the Messenger of God would combine the noon and mid-afternoon prayers, and the sundown and evening prayers, when he was in

Madinah at times when there was neither reason to be fearful of danger (for example, on account of being on the battlefield, in which case it might be necessary to combine prayers due to the demands of warfare), nor rain so heavy that it would have caused hardship for people to reach the mosque for both prayers. When Ibn ʿAbbās was asked, "Why did he do that?" he replied, "In order not to cause undue hardship for his people." We also read in both *Ṣaḥīḥ Muslim* and *Ṣaḥīḥ al-Bukhārī* on the authority of Ibn ʿAbbās that in Madinah the Messenger of God would combine the noon and mid-afternoon prayers by performing eight *rakʿahs*, and the sundown and evening prayers by performing seven *rakʿahs*. It was on this basis that Imam Aḥmad ibn Taymiyyah, who was a qualified practitioner of ijtihad, (independent reasoning and interpretation), ruled that it is permissible to combine prayers without being on a journey or having some extenuating circumstance or condition provided that it does not become a habit. How much more permissible will this practice be, then, in cases involving suffering, need or necessity?

15 Ibn ʿAbd al-Barr states in *al-Tamhīd*, vol. 8, p.386, "Have you not heard what Abū ʿUbaydah said to ʿUmar, may God have mercy on them both, saying, 'Do you flee from the decree of God?' to which ʿUmar replied, 'I flee from the decree of God to the decree of God.'"

16 *Fatḥ al-Bārī*, vol. 13, p. 34.

17 Abdullah Yusuf Ali renders the phrase as, 'If then any one transgresses the prohibition against you, transgress ye likewise against him.'

18 A *ḥadīth qudsī* is an utterance of God on the lips of the Prophet, which is not found in the Qur'an.

19 Narrated by Muslim in *Ṣaḥīḥ*, The Book of Righteousness, Relations with Others, and Morals, the section on the prohibition of injustice, hadith no. 2577.

20 Narrated by Abū Yaʿlā al-Mūṣilī, *Musnad ʿAbd Allāh ibn Masʿūd*, hadith no. 5586.

21 *Sunan al-Tirmidhī*, The Book of Righteousness and Relations with Others and Morals, hadith no. 2007.

22 *Ṣaḥīḥ Muslim*, The Book of Righteousness, Relations with Others, and Morals, hadith no. 2593.

23 *Saḥīḥ al-Bukhārī*, hadith no. 2310.

24 *Saḥīḥ al-Bukhārī*, hadith no. 6119.

25 *Ṣaḥīḥ Muslim*, hadith no. 2585, the section dealing with Muslims' compassion for one another and their mutual support.

26 *Ṣaḥīḥ Muslim*, The Book of Righteousness, Relations with Others, and Morals, hadith no. 2586.

27 *Sunan al-Bayhaqī*, hadith no. 19018.

28 *The Musnad* of Imam Aḥmad ibn Ḥanbal, hadith no. 16745.

29 See *Mustadrak al-Ḥākim*, The Book of Sales, hadith no. 2166.

30 *Ṣaḥīḥ Muslim*, hadith no. 2699.

31 *Musnad al-Shihāb*, hadith no. 176.

32 Narrated by al-Ṭabarānī in *al-Muᶜjam al-Awsaṭ*, hadith no. 4749.

33 *Saḥīḥ al-Bukhārī*, hadith no. 6552.

34 *Mustadrak al-Ḥākim*.

35 In explanation of this verse, Muhammad Asad notes that although this verse refers primarily to oaths relating to divorce (see 2:226), it also has a general import. In this connection, he draws attention to the saying of the Prophet that, "If anyone takes a solemn oath [that he would do or refrain from doing such-and-such a thing], and thereupon realizes that something else would be a more righteous course, then let him do that which is more righteous, and let him break his oath and then atone for it" (Bukhārī and Muslim). Quoted in Asad, *The Message of the Qur'an*, p.49.

36 Related by Ibn Mājah in his *Sunan*, hadith no.46.

37 *Saḥīḥ al-Bukhārī*, the section on etiquette, hadith no. 5745.

38 *Saḥīḥ al-Bukhārī*, The Book of Faith and the Signs of Hypocrisy, hadith no. 33.

39 This statement of ᶜUmar's is recorded in three different books, including *al-Mustaṭraf* by al-Abshīnī and *Rabīᶜ al-Abrār wa Nuṣūṣ al-Akhyār* by al-Zamakhsharī.

40 For a detailed treatment of the issues involved here, see Abdul Hamid AbuSulayman, *Al-ᶜUnf wa Idārat al-Ṣirāᶜ al-Siyāsī fī al-Fikr al-Islāmī: Bayn al-Mabda' wa al-Khayār*; or its English translation, *Violence and the Management of Political Conflict in Islamic Thought: Between Principle and Choice*.

It is important to bear in mind here that more than fourteen hundred years ago, the Islamic vision of justice divided the world of human social and political relations into three spheres or 'abodes' – namely, the abode of peace (*dār al-salām*), the abode of covenant (*dār al-ᶜahd*), and the abode of war (*dār al-ḥarb*).

With respect to the Muslim community, the 'abode of peace' is 'the abode of Islam' – that is, the society whose members are subject to the rule of the Islamic state and whose relations are therefore characterized by harmony. It is not permissible for any group or individuals within this sphere to take the law in its or their hands, and should this take place, it is considered a criminal act to be deterred by the society. As for opposition to injustices, it must take place within the framework of the law and by legal means. If such means fail, it is legitimate for citizens to resort to nonviolent resistance, since they are not under obligation to obey any authority which is not founded on justice and the rule of law.

As for the relationship between the abode of peace, represented by the sovereign Islamic state in the contemporary political sense, and the outside world and its various political entities – it will take the form of either the abode of covenant or the abode of war. The abode of covenant is that community or sphere whose relationship with the sovereign Islamic state (the abode of peace) is based on a mutual agreement, which preserves and protects the rights of both parties, and in which both parties share common interests on the basis of consent and fair dealings. This type of covenant, which assumes peaceful, honorable intentions on the part of both or all signatories, helps to achieve stability. Otherwise, we have a situation in which parties to the so-called covenant are actually lying in wait for one another. In the context of our modern-day situation, the abode of covenant finds its parallel in the role played by international agreements and treaties and the United Nations.

As for political units or states that commit aggression against other states – that is, against the abode of peace and the abode of covenant – and cannot be persuaded by peaceful, diplomatic means to retreat from their aggression and injustices, they thereby become the abode of war, that is, enemy states. When this happens, the abode of peace and/or the abode of covenant that has been the victim of the aggression is entitled to employ whatever means are necessary and appropriate, including war, if required in order to bring the initial aggression to an end. However, the teachings of Islam stipulate that the response to aggression must not be excessive, and that whatever violence is employed in retaliation must target only those in power.

Operating on the basis of the law of the jungle, the materialist modern world has established the self-centered nationalistic state in place of the Islamic concept of the abode of peace, and replaced the abode of covenant with a new world order based on subjugation, tyranny, unequally balanced treaties, and unwarranted pressures – while making use of the United Nations (the activities of the Security Council and power politics) as a means of allowing the powerful to dominate the weak. Moreover, as we are seeing in many areas of the world through devastating, unjust wars by means of which the world's superpowers consolidate their ascendency over weak peoples (despite the fact that the United Nations Charter has declared war illegitimate), the abode of war is clearly a reality today. In fact, the super powers have even sought assistance from the United Nations in order to justify unwarranted aggression against third world powers and their oppressed populations.

41 Recorded by al-Tirmidhī and Ibn Mājah with a strong chain of transmission. Ibn al-Ghars declares it authentic, though some have claimed that it is weak.

Chapter II

1 *Sunan Abī Dāwūd*, hadith no. 5119.

2 *Sunan al-Nasā'ī al-Kubrā*, hadith no. 7830.

3 *Ṣaḥīḥ Muslim*, hadith no. 2578.

4 *Ṣaḥīḥ Muslim*, The Book of Righteousness, Relations with Others, and Morals, the section on the prohibition of injustice, hadith no. 2577.

5 *Ṣaḥīḥ al-Bukhārī*, hadith no. 2315.

6 A great deal has been written about the veracity of the Prophet Muhammad and the

truthfulness of the Islamic message. For a discussion of relevance to this theme, see my article entitled, 'Istidrāk ʿalā Ẓāhiriyat Ibn Ḥazm,' *Majallat al-Tajdīd*, 3 (1998). See also my introduction to *Ẓāhiriyat Ibn Ḥazm* (The Literalism of Ibn Ḥazm) by Dr. Anwar Khalid al-Zuʿbi, which, given its direct relevance to the credibility of the Qur'anic worldview, I have included it as Appendix II in the present volume with the title, 'Faith: A Matter of Reason, or the Miraculous?'

7 Among the Qur'anic concepts that are frequently misunderstood and misused and which therefore need to be rescued from sophistries, scholastic complications, and political ax-grinding, are those having to do with the way people understand and relate to the events in their lives. One such concept is that of 'divine decree' (*al-qaḍā'*) and 'fate' (*al-qadar*). If understood in light of the way in which they are treated in the Qur'an, these concepts are simple and straightforward. Consequently, the best way to understand the meaning of these terms is to refer directly to passages in the Qur'an in which they occur. An examination of these terms' use in the Qur'an itself makes clear that they have nothing to do with the human will and the responsibility human beings have been given to be responsible stewards of the earth; in other words, they have no relevance to the controversy over so-called predestination (*al-jabr*) and free will (*al-ikhtiyār*).

The Arabic term translated as 'divine decree' (*al-qaḍā'*) has to do with the divine affirmation of what is appropriate, good, and required of human beings, be it an action we are called upon to perform, or something we are required to refrain from. As for our response to such affirmations, it remains dependent on the human will itself. The Qur'anic term rendered as fate (*al-qadar*) has to do with the creation and what God has deposited therein by way of innate tendencies and unchanging laws and patterns. These tendencies, laws, and patterns constitute the universe in which we live, and which determines the limits of our abilities and potentials.

None of this, however, constitutes a denial of the efficacy of the human will. On the contrary, it is we who determine our own fates, and it is the human will that takes human action in this direction or that. A willful, ungrateful, unbelieving individual, who insists on the pursuit of injustice, aggression, and corruption, will refuse to listen to sound advice and will not submit to guidance. Such a person wrongs himself: "And it is not We who will be doing wrong unto them, but it is they who will have wronged themselves" (*sūrah al-Zukhruf*, 43:76).

8 It is not possible to understand the human will and its choices solely on the basis of what a person knows, understands, and feels; rather, in order to understand human will and choice, it is necessary to postulate the existence of an unseen, metaphysical dimension that, by its nature, goes beyond human logic. The secret to this metaphysical dimension may lie in the divine spirit that has been breathed into human beings. The Qur'an tells us that when God was about to create Adam, He said to the angels,

"and when I have formed him fully and breathed into him of My spirit, fall down before him in prostration!" (*sūrah al-Ḥijr*, 15:29). It goes without saying, of course, that God alone possesses a fully independent, unrestricted will: "...when He wills a thing to be, He but says unto it, 'Be' – and it is" (*sūrah Āl ʿImrān*, 3:47); and, "...when [God] judges, there is no power that could repel His judgment..." (*sūrah al-Raʿd*, 13:41). The degree of free will and autonomy that God has granted to human beings is one of the qualifications God has given us for the task of stewardship, since it is a purposeful, moral task that requires the freedom to decide and entails responsibility for decisions made and actions undertaken.

It will be clear from the foregoing that the issue of human free will has to do with a dimension of existence that goes beyond human knowledge, and which is related in some way to the spirit God breathes into human beings upon their creation:

> Limitless in His glory is He who has created opposites in whatever the earth produces, and in men's own selves, and in that of which [as yet] they have no knowledge. (*sūrah Yā Sīn*, 36:36)
>
> ...Indeed, unmindful hast thou been of this [Day of Judgment]; but now We have lifted from thee thy veil, and sharp is thy sight today! (*sūrah Qāf*, 50:22)
>
> And they will ask thee about [the nature of] divine inspiration. Say: "This inspiration [comes] at my Sustainer's behest; and [you cannot understand its nature, O men, since] you have been granted very little of [real] knowledge." (*sūrah al-Isrā'*, 17:85)

The human will is created and operates within a created world. How, then, can it be endowed with freedom of choice and burdened with responsibility and ultimate accountability for such choices as though these choices were completely free and autonomous?

Clearly, then, it is impossible to comprehend this freedom and responsibility and the fairness inherent therein through human logic and knowledge alone. Rather, one also needs to have confidence that God is both just and merciful, and that within the limits of the laws of the cosmos (*al-qadar*), we possess the freedom and ability to make choices and decisions and are thus responsible for the decisions we make. As we have seen, the question of how the human will could be created yet be autonomous, or how such a created will could justly be held accountable for its choices and actions, pertains to the realm of the unseen and a logic that goes beyond the merely human. This question, on the moral or ethical level, is the counterpart to the logical conundrum of how existence could have arisen out of nonexistence. We observe the phenomenon of human freedom and responsibility, and we experience its effects – yet without being able to comprehend it with our finite minds, since it operates on the basis of a logic that goes beyond human reason, belonging as it does to the world of the spirit and the unseen.

The Qur'an depicts for us the scene in which, out of arrogance and envy of the capacities for knowledge, creativity and action that God had bestowed on Adam, Iblīs chose of his own free will to go astray and become evil. In so doing, Iblīs broke with the other angels, who had accepted the divine decree concerning Adam, trusting in God's perfect wisdom and obeying the divine command to bow down to Adam.

Hence, it was Iblīs' own choice to disobey God and to act instead out of arrogance and self-importance, thereby becoming evil, corrupt, and an instigator of corruption among others. God Almighty says:

> And lo! Thy Sustainer said unto the angels: "Behold, I am about to create mortal man out of sounding clay, out of dark slime transmuted; and when I have formed him fully and breathed into him of My spirit, fall down before him in prostration!" Thereupon the angels prostrated themselves, all of them together, save Iblīs: he refused to be among those who prostrated themselves. Said He: "O Iblīs! what is thy reason for not being among those who have prostrated themselves?" [Iblīs] replied, "It is not for me to prostrate myself before mortal man whom Thou hast created out of sounding clay, out of dark slime transmuted!" (*sūrah al-Ḥijr*, 15:28–33)

> [And God] said: "What has kept thee from prostrating thyself when I commanded thee?" Answered [Iblīs], "I am better than he: Thou hast created me out of fire, whereas him Thou hast created out of clay." [God] said: "Down with thee, then, from this [state] – for it is not meet for thee to show arrogance here! Go forth, then: verily, among the humiliated shalt thou be!" Said [Iblīs]: "Grant me a respite till the Day when all shall be raised from the dead." [And God] replied: "Verily, thou shalt be among those who are granted a respite." (*sūrah al-Aʿrāf*, 7:12–15)

Thus, we see that Iblīs was not created evil; rather, it was he who chose freely – out of arrogance, conceit, and envy – to disobey, to exalt himself, and to follow the destructive path of revenge against Adam and his progeny who, unlike the angels, have been placed on earth as God's stewards and given the gifts and capacities required in order to fulfill this role. And just as Iblīs chose of his own free will to tread the path of error and disobedience, human beings likewise choose freely to follow the path of wrongdoing, error, corruption, and aggression by paying heed to Satan's deceitful whisperings and suggestions and giving in to his temptations. It is by virtue of our own freely made choices that goodness, righteousness, justice, compassion, and peace reign in our lives – or, conversely, that our thoughts and actions are tainted by corruption, evil, injustice, cruelty, and hostility: "...And [by all their sinning] they did no harm unto Us – but [only] against their own selves did they sin" (*sūrah al-Baqarah*, 2:57); and, "...It is not God who does them wrong, but it is they who are wronging themselves" (*sūrah Āl ᶜImrān*, 3:117).

Another issue that touches upon our relationship with the world of the unseen is that of the trials and tests we are sent by God, whether through blessing or through hardship. As we have seen, human beings have been granted an autonomous will and the capacity to make meaningful choices within the limits set for them through the laws of the created universe: "God does not burden any human being with more than he is well able to bear: in his favour shall be whatever good he does, and against him whatever evil he does...." (*sūrah al-Baqarah*, 2:286).

In this way does He cause many a one to go astray, just as He guides many a one aright: but none does He cause thereby to go astray save the iniquitous,. All of this manifests some aspect of the divine wisdom of which human beings realize a part, although human knowledge and logic can never encompass the entirety of the spiritual world and its mysteries. The Qur'anic account of Moses and the wise man (*sūrah al-Kahf*, 18:64–82) illustrates clearly the limitations of human knowledge and the human ability to perceive the divine wisdom and purposes being worked out through life's varied circumstances: "...It may well be that you hate a thing the while it is good for you, and it may well be that you love a thing the while it is bad for you: and God knows, whereas you do not know" (*sūrah al-Baqarah*, 2:216).

Thoughtful reflection on the Qur'anic story of creation makes clear that suffering and trial in a person's life occur on the basis of a divine decree. When Adam, of his own free will, chose to listen to the prompting of Iblīs and ate of the tree that God had forbidden to him, God caused him to descend from the primordial garden and the world of the spirit to earth and the world of matter. In this latter world, he would experience both the spirit in its pristine loftiness and matter in its crudity and baseness, for in this way his will would be put to the test through trial, sometimes through blessings, and other times through tribulation. If through blessing, the test would reveal whether he would respond with trust, faith, good works, and gratitude, or with unbelief, ingratitude, wastefulness, and niggardliness toward others; if through tribulation, the test would reveal whether the response was one of faith, trust, and patient endurance, or one of denial, bitterness, distress, and fearfulness. As God declares in the Qur'an:

"And [as for thee], O Adam, dwell thou and thy wife in this garden, and eat, both of you, whatever you may wish; but do not approach this one tree, lest you become evildoers!" Thereupon Satan whispered unto the two with a view to making them conscious of their nakedness, of which [hitherto] they had been unaware... (*sūrah al-Aʿrāf*, 7:19–20)

and thereupon We said, "O Adam! Verily, this is a foe unto thee and thy wife: so let him not drive the two of you out of this garden and render thee unhappy." (*sūrah Ṭā Hā*, 20:117)

But Satan caused them both to stumble therein, and thus brought about the loss of their erstwhile state. And so We said: "Down with you, [and be henceforth] enemies unto one another; and on earth you shall have your abode and your livelihood for a while!" (*sūrah al-Baqarah*, 2:36)

"He who has created death as well as life, so that He might put you to a test [and thus show] which of you is best in conduct,..." (*sūrah al-Mulk*, 67:2)

The foregoing verses from the Qur'an make clear that the human will is the means by which we are tested through blessing and affliction, good and evil, enjoyment and suffering, ease and hardship. The situation might be schematized through the following diagram:

Spirit ➜ disobedience ➜ descent ➜ material world ➜ spirit + matter ➜ fate (*al-qadar*) – divine decree (*al-qaḍā'*), that is, divine guidance – human will (choice) ➜ testing through blessing (praise, good works and gratitude, or wastefulness, arrogance, self-reliance, and stinginess toward others) + testing through hardship (contentment, praise, and long-suffering, or bitterness, fear, anxiety, and unbelief) ➜ faith or unbelief ➜ happiness or misery.

9 *Saḥīḥ al-Bukhārī*, The Book of Sales, the section pertaining to what a man earns and working with his own hands, hadith no. 1966.

10 Narrated by Abū Yaʿlā al-Mūṣalī in his *Musnad*, hadith no. 3370.

11 *Al-Muʿjam al-Ṣaghīr*, hadith no. 861.

12 Narrated by Imam Aḥmad in his *Musnad*, hadith no. 13004.

13 *Muṣannaf ʿAbd al-Razzāq*, hadith no. 5104.

14 Narrated by Muslim in his *Ṣaḥīḥ*, The Book of Faith, hadith no. 91.

15 *Mustadrak al-Ḥākim*, hadith no. 7371.

16 *Saḥīḥ al-Bukhārī*, Book 72, hadith no. 779.

17 In other words, God loves to see His servants nicely dressed. Narrated by Aḥmad, *Musnad.*

18 Narrated by Abū Dāwūd, *Sunan Abu Dāwūd,* Book 33, hadith no. 4151.

19 *Muṣannaf ʿAbd al-Razzāq,* hadith no. 5104.

20 *Sunan al-Nasā'ī al-Kubrā,* hadith no. 9352. *Katam* is a plant used to dye the hair black.

Chapter IV

1 The era of the Companions' rule was, in essence, an extension of the Prophetic era in its thought, practices, relations, and arrangements. In addition, it was marked by interpretations that were dictated by the need to deal with the major changes that had been brought about, on one hand, by the death of the Messenger of God and the end of the era of divine revelation – and, on the other hand, by the Islamic conquests. Arab tribalism subsequently took over government and management of the state, thereby contributing to the political, economic, and social deviations of the Umayyad era and the ruinous battles that took place with the Madinah School.

2 For a discussion of the issues pertaining to the crises of thought and will in the history of the Muslim community, see AbdulHamid AbuSulayman, *Crisis in the Muslim Mind.*

Chapter V

1 That is, before the sun has risen and the heat of the day is upon them.

Appendix I

1 From here we begin to teach and learn: The requirements of cultural construction.

Appendix II

1 "Ta'ammulāt fī Ẓāhiriyat Ibn Ḥazm wa Iʿjāz al-Risālah al-Muḥammadiyyah," *Majallat al-Tajdīd* 3, pp.167–72.

2 Ijtihad (independent reasoning) is the effort exerted by a suitably qualified scholar of jurisprudence to arrive at an accurate conceptualization of the divine will and the means by which to apply this will in a given age and under given circumstances based on Muslim legal sources (the Qur'an, the Hadith, analogical deduction, and consensus); as such, Ijtihad is the effort exerted by such a scholar to derive a legal ruling from Muslim legal sources, and to reach certainty on questions of an ambiguous nature.